AUTISM AND COMPUTERS

MAXIMIZING INDEPENDENCE THROUGH TECHNOLOGY

VALERIE HERSKOWITZ

authorHOUSE®

AuthorHouse™
1663 Liberty Drive
Bloomington, IN 47403
www.authorhouse.com
Phone: 1-800-839-8640

First published by AuthorHouse 5/6/2009

ISBN: 978-1-4389-8114-7 (sc)
ISBN: 978-1-4389-8115-4 (hc)

Library of Congress Control Number: 2009904410

Printed in the United States of America
Bloomington, Indiana

This book is printed on acid-free paper.

TABLE OF CONTENTS

DEDICATION

To the light that illuminates my path. To the one that leads me through life and helps me to understand my life's purpose, I dedicate this book to my son, Blake.

Over the past few months, since I have given up the responsibilities of running a hectic therapy center and dedicated my time to this book and other projects that have kept me more at home, I have rediscovered my best pal, Blake. He has always been the spirit in everything that I do in the name of autism. More recently, however, my relationship with him has taken on a new dimension: Blake is now at the age of young adulthood. And while he is still a child in many ways, parts of him illustrate an aged soul. Our connection is not simply one in which I play the role of his mother, caretaker, and teacher, but he has also been and continues to be there for me. Call it co-dependency or even symbiosis—whatever the psychological world may name it—but Blake nurtures me as much as I nurture him.

Aside from the housekeeping tasks that are Blake's responsibility, he seems to understand the power of a smile, the effect of a hug, and just important it is for me to share in the pure joy he receives from life's simple pleasures— things like a bubble bath, a ride in the car, or listening to music. Because of his frequent demonstrations of delight and pleasure, I have also learned to derive bliss from things as uncomplicated as a warm shower at the end of the day, a kiss from my husband, or Blake's wonderful laughter. Blake is my teacher as much as I am his. He continually provides the avenues that lead me to comprehend the true meaning of life itself. Blake is a constant reminder of what I continually need to strive for.

Recently, the parents of a six-year old boy with autism came to see me in my office. They were there to discuss what interventions I could recommend in order to increase their son's communication skills. The boy used no systematic method to express himself.

They talked about their son's frustrated behaviors as a result of his inability to get his point across. I noticed that the parents were quite distressed by the fact that their child was basically locked in his own head, unable to tell anyone what he wanted or how he felt. It was obvious that this child was bright in many ways, so I mentioned to the parents that I had a great deal of empathy for their son. I told them that it must be very sad for him to want something but not be able to tell anyone.

I asked the parents what communication methods they had attempted in the past, such as verbal behavior, sign language, picture systems, or technology-based systems.

Initially, they responded as I suspected, mentioning that they had attempted speech therapy to teach their son verbal communication skills. Obviously, this training had been unsuccessful. When he had been in a pre-school for children with autism, he had been exposed to a modified picture system. Later, they enrolled him in a private school which frowned on picture systems and attempted verbal and sign methods. These techniques also failed. Now, the child was past the age of six and had no real way to convey his thoughts.

I have had similar conversations with many parents throughout the years, so what they told me hardly came as a surprise. It was what they said next that rendered me speechless.

When I asked the parents why they waited so long to consult with a specialist, they said that they had thought he would be cured of the autism by now. I assumed this was because they were undergoing biomedical treatments under a doctor's care. But no, that wasn't the case. They had not been involved with biomedical interventions. "Not even the gluten and casein-free diet?" I asked.

I have also met several families who have felt strongly that their child would be restored to optimal health through prayer and belief. But these parents held no religious convictions that led them to believe he would be cured.

Finally, I stopped playing "Twenty Questions," and they told me that they believed their child would have received stem cell treatment by now, and that would have healed him. It was the first time I had heard such a thing. The parents still hoped that this type of medical intervention would be available eventually, but they finally realized that it was time to begin an aggressive program of communication training.

After I regained my ability to speak, I explained my thoughts on this subject. I mentioned that I'm a firm believer in all types of interventions, including biomedical treatments. I feel that prayer and spirituality increases healing for ourselves, as well as for our children with issues. And I believe that all of the current research will eventually lead us to the cause of autism and, ultimately, the cure.

But—and this is a big "BUT"—should we put all of our energy into the hope that our children will turn out all right? Should we put every ounce of our dreams into possibilities that we cannot control? Or should we deal with our children and the world as they are today?

I feel strongly that along with prayers, research, and medical treatments, we must try to do what we can to help our children become all they can be. The ultimate goal for every individual with a developmental disability is to reach a state of maximum independence. While each person's level of "maximum" independence will be different, the objective is the same: To help our children grow up to be as self-sufficient as possible. That means figuring out what the world is about today and what it will be about when our children are adults, targeting all of our objectives in that direction.

Those objectives are what this book is all about. You will understand what your child needs to know *today*, and you will get a glimpse into their needs for *tomorrow*. You will learn that the way for these individuals to reach the top is through accessing technology. Why? Because technology is here today, and it will be here tomorrow in an even greater capacity.

Technology offers unbelievable opportunities for individuals with developmental disabilities. There are applications on the market now that can help our children immediately, and there are some on the horizon that will be there for them when they reach adulthood. It's never too early to get started on the technology bandwagon. So, whether your child is 2 or 22, or even 42, technology holds the answers for him or her to lead a more self-reliant future.

This book will describe how individuals with autism and other developmental challenges take to technology like fish to water. I will help you learn how to set up a Computer-Based Intervention (CBI) lab in your own home or in your child's school environment. I will describe different augmentative devices that help individuals with low verbal skills become effective communicators. When you finish this book, you will have the information you need to start your child on the road to becoming technologically inclined.

What happened to the six-year old boy? The story has a happy ending. His parents realized that it was time to get going with an aggressive communication and skill training program. He started Computer-Based Intervention immediately and, as predicted, quickly increased his ability to learn language and other skills. He is in the pre-training stages for a communication device. He is most definitely happier, less frustrated, and on his way to a brighter future.

His parents still hope for the day when science discovers the cure for autism, and so do I. But in the meantime, we're helping their son unlock his world using the key that we have available today—technology.

CHAPTER ONE:

WELCOME TO THE NEW WORLD

*"How wonderful it is that nobody need wait a single
moment before starting to improve the world."*
                                                    -Anne Frank

The statistics are mind-blowing. You've probably heard
the ratio: 1 out of 150 individuals have been diagnosed
with autism. Did you know that this adds up to more than
1,500,000 individuals in the United States alone? Add to this
staggering number close to two million in India and another
one million in China, as well as millions more around the
world. And that's just autism. The statistics actually reveal
that 10% of the population has some sort of disability.

Many of these individuals are still children, but eventually
they grow into adults. A plethora of problems and issues
occur as a result and will continue to develop as more
children enter into their older years.

THE HOUSING PROBLEM

The first issue that needs to be addressed is housing. Even
now, there is a critical housing shortage for adults with
disabilities. Talk to any parent of a child who is above the
age of 22, and you will get an earful. Recently, I spoke with
six families in my area of South Florida who were trying to
place their older adolescent children into a facility that would
both educate them and provide living space. One mother
mentioned that all that was offered to her was a group
home in the middle of nowhere. No special services were

1

offered and no opportunities for social development. These families ended up donating $100,000 each to a residential school two hours away from their homes in order for the facility to convert an old restaurant into a living space. And that doesn't include the monthly fees. How many people can afford to do that? Not many, I imagine.

So, what will happen in five, 10, or even 15 years from now when the one out of 150 individuals diagnosed with autism become adults?

During the Reagan years, institutions were disbanded because they became known as places that warehoused these individuals. But then, the idea of the group home was born, in which three to six individuals are housed in certain communities. Service workers either live in the home or work in shifts. During the day, the individuals are transported to day habilitation centers where they engage in some sort of mini-employment activity. Some individuals are able to be trained to work in businesses and industry in the community at large.

The concept works well for some. However, there are laws in many communities that require group homes to be at least 1,000 feet apart from each other. In addition, some neighborhoods are forbidden to have more than 10% disabled people in the population. This is known as the 10% density rule. Many advocacy groups are fighting these rulings. They feel that it is discriminatory to forbid individuals with disabilities to live near each other.

I guess the reasoning behind the 10% density rule is to ensure that neighborhoods do not become ghettos for the disabled. Some people are afraid that their property values will decrease, while others feel that it is important for individuals with disabilities to assimilate within the community at large. No one size fits all. And as mentioned previously, there are so few spots in these homes available that families with adult children must often keep their loved one at home with them even though they may not be able to provide the proper care.

Recently, I have been to conferences that address these issues, and I see many parents who are well into their 60's and 70's still trying their best to care for their adult children with disabilities at home. They simply have no better place for them to go.

PRODUCTIVITY AFTER HIGH SCHOOL

This brings us to our second issue: Productivity after high school. In most cases, high school doesn't end at the age of 18 for those with autism. Most parents utilize the system until their child is 22. This additional time gives families the ability to plan for their loved one's life once school is over. While there are some individuals who are able to acquire jobs in the community, there are many more who cannot.

Perhaps in your own town, you may know certain businesses that have hired those with autism. Perhaps it's your local supermarket, drugstore, or movie theatre. Occasionally, I have heard about retail stores offering stock positions in the back where the employee is not in the vicinity of the customers. Once in awhile, offices will hire them to do filing or copy work. Often, these individuals will attend vocational training schools and actually be able to learn a trade. Finding a place in the community willing to hire them, however, is often a difficult task. Yes, there are some individuals who are able to be productive and assimilate into the culture around them. But for most, this possibility just doesn't exist.

Having worked with so many individuals with autism, it is my firm belief that every single one of them can be trained to be productive—high functioning, low functioning, and every place in the middle. And often their abilities revolve around the use of computers and technology.

COMING TO TERMS WITH REALITY

I know that if you're a parent of a young child with autism, you may have a hard time envisioning a time when you will have to deal with this issue—especially if your child is under the age of ten. You may imagine a time in the future in which your child will be living apart from you, on his or her own, and able to function without assistance or support. Or you may have arrived at the time in your life when you realize your child *will* need some sort of support as an adult, but you have yet to figure out how that support will be delivered.

When most parents come to accept that their child will be dependent in some way for his or her entire life, they just assume that their child will continue to live with them. Usually, parents are fairly young during this stage. They're in good health and still working. The child may still be young enough to handle, and parents are still focused on the here and now.

But somewhere between pre-puberty and adolescence, some kids go through a disruptive behavioral period. Perhaps they exhibit aggressive tendencies or self-injurious behaviors. Sometimes, if the behaviors escalate to a great degree, parents may feel like their lives have spun out of control. The child may even be taller and stronger than the parents by this time. The mother may become a victim to her own child's rage and hormonal-induced aggressive behavior.

It's often at this time that a parent asks: "If I'm unable to handle my child at this stage of the game, what's going to happen when he's older?" Through medical and behavioral interventions and the ending of the puberty stage, these behaviors will mitigate. The experience will still leave its mark on the psyche of the parents, however, and the question of what to do with the child in the near future lives on in their minds.

There are other scenarios that occur. Perhaps one of the parents becomes ill or just the onset of middle age brings the future into question. While their friends are researching retirement strategies or planning that long-awaited cruise, parents of children with special needs wonder if they'll ever experience empty-nest syndrome. Adding to the stress, these parents may become sandwiched between caring for their adolescent special needs child while also dealing with their own aged parents. It feels like the proverbial treadmill moves faster and faster, and the future doesn't seem all that distant anymore.

"Who will care for my child when he becomes an adult?" "Where will he live?" "What will she do?" "Who will look after her when I'm gone?" Unable to continue to squash these thoughts away, parents often lie awake at night pondering their options.

THE COSTS

How many of you realize how much money it costs for an individual with developmental disabilities to live in the family home once there is no one to take care of them? If you do the math, the price tag can run as high as $70,000 a year. That's in today's terms. By the time most of these children are adults, the cost will probably exceed $100,000. I'll bet you're surprised. I know I was shocked when I first heard the number. How could that possibly be?

Of course, the number varies greatly depending on many factors: the family's lifestyle, whether or not the house has been paid off, the extent of care that the individual requires, etc. No matter the situation, however, there's nothing cheap about it.

And who pays these costs? During the period of time that this book is being written, the U.S. economy is, to be graphic, in the toilet. Government programs are being slashed on both the federal and state levels. Every day, newspapers around the country contain articles discussing drastic cuts that affect the disabled population. I have spoken to administrators who operate state-financed group homes that have housed some individuals for over a decade. With all of the government programs being cut back to the bone, they cannot continue to house these people in the future. Adults with developmental disabilities who have no family and no ability to take care of themselves are being displaced. I don't even know where they go; I'm afraid to ask.

For parents who don't have children with special needs, there appears to be a clear track to follow: You raise your children in your family home until they reach approximately 18 years old. Then, they usually continue with some post-high school education or training with the goal of learning a trade or acquiring the education to be employable in society by the time they reach their early to mid-20's. Of course, there are several variations on this theme, but the point is that we basically assume that our financial and caretaking responsibilities to these children will have an end point in our lifetime. Then, we can focus on ourselves and/or our aging parents.

The path for parents of special needs children is not so clear. In fact, it's murky at best. There are some children who are high functioning enough to follow a modified version of the above scenario. But individuals with autism are really not in that category. *Not yet anyway.*

Whether you're a parent of a child with autism or another developmental disability or a family member, friend, or professional, I'm sure you feel strongly that we must address these issues immediately. We don't have the luxury of waiting another decade to figure out how we're going to house our children when they're adults. And we must do more than put a roof over their heads and food in their stomachs. We must provide opportunities for all individuals with autism to live happy, productive lives. Individuals with autism have normal life spans. That means that most will live well beyond the time that their parents are gone. Some may have siblings, but others do not. And is it fair to burden siblings? No, it isn't. We must figure a better way.

◆　◆　◆　◆　◆

A Story for the Future

Rachel wakes up this morning as she does every morning due to the slight vibration that she feels within her mattress. It's a subtle but distinct feeling—not startling, but enough to rouse her from slumber. After a very comfortable night's sleep, thanks to the posture-conforming bed, Rachel spends a minute or two before sauntering into the bathroom. She touches the bathroom mirror, which then tells her what she needs to do for the day. "Today is Monday," Rachel hears. "Eight A.M., time to dress. Eight-thirty, time for breakfast. Nine A.M., wait for transportation. Nine-thirty, begin work." The mirror rattles off the first sequence of activities that define Rachel's Monday morning.

In the bathroom, Rachel accesses the touchpad next to the bathtub. She presses the "on" button, and the tub begins to fill with water which is pre-set to a specific temperature. The touchpad allows for changes to the temperature, but this feature has been disabled. The faucet shuts off automatically when the tub is full, and Rachel steps into the tub to wash. Fifteen minutes later, the tub begins to empty, cuing Rachel to exit the tub. She pulls a warmed towel from the heated towel rack, dries herself, and proceeds to her room to get dressed.

On the closet door, Rachel pushes a button for Monday, and within a few moments, several items of clothing are projected from the closet. Rachel dons the pre-selected clothing items and proceeds into the kitchen.

"I'm hungry," Rachel thinks to herself. Happily, she enters the kitchen knowing that her favorite breakfast foods will be available, thanks to the fact that the refrigerator reminded her to order the products last Friday via the touchpad in the kitchen. While she is eating breakfast, she hears her video phone ring. "Mom!" she attempts to say with her mouth full of cereal.

"Good morning, Rachel. I see you're getting ready for work. I like your outfit. You look really stylish today," her mother remarks.

"Thank you," Rachel responds.

"Okay, honey. Talk to you after work," Rachel's mother says.

After breakfast, Rachel grabs the belongings she needs to take with her to work. One of the items is her PDA. She turns it on to check her responsibilities this morning at work. With a quick touch, she views the pictorial representations and begins to mentally prepare for her morning.

Rachel walks outside to the bus stop on the corner. She checks her PDA to remind her of the correct bus she needs to take to work. Bus 22, on time as usual, is coming down the street. Rachel enters the bus, slides her prepaid card in the slot, and grabs her usual seat at the front of the bus. She listens carefully for the speaker to announce her stop, which will leave her outside of her office.

Rachel enters the room in her office where she is assigned to work. Her job involves data records management. As she enters the office, her boss greets her via the computer. Rachel sees him on her screen. "Hi, Rachel", her boss says. "How are you today? Let's get started on today's workload." Through the live streaming video, Rachel is assisted through her daily work tasks. Her boss oversees her, as well as several other individuals throughout the day even though he doesn't work in the same office. Actually, he doesn't even work in the same city. Rachel's office is a satellite center for the business.

So, what is this? An episode from *The Jetsons*? My father, an avid *Star Trek* fan, would probably think that I stole this vignette from that series. But the truth is that this is actually a reality-based hypothetical story of what the world could be like in the near future. I based my examples on technology that is already being utilized in homes around the world or has been invented but not yet incorporated. I will be discussing these inventions in future chapters in this book.

If you close your eyes for a minute, could you visualize yourself as the character, Rachel? Could you imagine for a moment that your day started in much the same way that Rachel's began? Would it ease your morning routine to be awakened gently by vibrations in a mattress that had given you a good night's sleep because it electronically conformed to your body all through the night? How would it be to have a mirror that tells you your schedule or a bath that fills automatically with the water set to the exact temperature that you enjoy?

I don't know about you, but I could really use the high tech refrigerator that automatically signals when I'm out of certain foods and the touchpad in the kitchen that makes it effortless to order these items. But now, imagine that it's five, 10, or 15 years from now. Still keeping your eyes closed, visualize that the person in the story is your child who has been diagnosed with autism. Does it seem impossible to you at this point that your child with autism could be able to live in the manner described in the story?

The truth is that the character I created, Rachel, does have autism. She is twenty-six years old, and she lives in a hypothetical community with many other individuals with developmental disabilities. She has her own modified condo-style unit and a job in the data management center of an administrative office. She has plenty of support when needed, social activities, and a lot of contact with her family who lives in a private home nearby. This community may be hypothetical today, but it will be the reality in the not so distant future.

Though this scenario was created in my own mind and may sound far-fetched, it's actually my version of what is possible for our children's futures. Rachel lives in a community that provides both appropriate housing and productivity fulfillment. This community is composed of adult individuals with varying degrees of developmental disabilities. The community offers a variety of living arrangements based on the needs of each individual. Rachel lives in a condo-style unit. Because of the technological innovations that have been installed in her unit, she is able to manage certain daily living tasks on her own.

Others in the community are unable to live quite as independently as Rachel. Some live in a dormitory where there are caretakers. But even those who require maximum assistance are able to help themselves in many situations. These other individuals also work in the community, and each and every one of them has a purpose and offers something to the system. The community itself has been designed so that the residents are essential to the daily operations. Every job requires training, and this is provided within the community structure.

This story is not a pipe dream. It is actually in the process of being developed. It's a logical and realistic solution to the problem of where and how the scores of individuals with developmental disabilities will live out their adult lives in the near future.

Getting Ready for the Future

As a speech pathologist for the past 30 years, I have worked with many individuals who have a developmental issue—for the most part within the autism spectrum. I have had the opportunity to see my "kids" grow up and develop. Though no two individuals are the same, I feel that each and every one of them will be able to achieve some level of independence and some level of productivity. There is one very essential element, however, that I believe is necessary in order for these individuals to reach their potential: Technology training. If the main goal is to help these individuals reach their maximum potential, exposing our children to all of the technological advantages available today will give them the greatest opportunity to reach that goal.

The world of today, and certainly the world of tomorrow, is jam-packed with technological innovations that can greatly enhance the ability for these individuals to live more independently. Every day, I discover new applications for products that are on the market which could be used with the developmentally disabled population.

We must create communities that will incorporate housing which provides these technological advances in order to ensure that our children will live as independently as possible. Within these communities, we must create jobs for these individuals and social opportunities that provide a sense of purpose and a reason to live.

The Time is Now

I'm sure that many of you have had the experience of purchasing a piece of hardware or software, after which you scratched your head, unable to figure out the device or program. Next, you may have attempted to install the equipment or software following the directions that came with it. Perhaps you just couldn't get it going at all. Finally, you called your 10 or 12-year old typical child, and voila! Within five minutes, the kid had the whole thing operating perfectly without even having read the manual or directions. You were no doubt thrilled that you were in business but frustrated that your young child was able to figure it out in the blink of an eye when you were still scratching your head after an hour.

Of course, we all know the reason: These kids have grown up with computers and other technologies. Some of them can't remember a time when computers, cell phones, or cable TV didn't exist. You may love telling stories of when your Dad came home with the family's first color television or how you used to type term papers on a typewriter using information from a set of encyclopedias that were real books. Similarly, did you have to help set up your parents' first VCR? Or perhaps your mother and father still had dial phones well into the late 1990s.

The point is that when you grow up with something, it comes naturally to you. If you're a baby boomer, your parents may have sent you over the summer for typing lessons when you were in Junior High School (now called Middle School.) Did you have to send your kids for typing lessons? Of course, not. They used word processors to complete their third grade book reports.

So, if you want your child with autism to be able to embrace all of the technological applications that will be available to him or her when at adulthood, it's imperative to begin training today. It doesn't matter whether your child is only two years old. It's time to begin. And if your child is older, that's okay, too. You probably weren't a baby when you got your first home computer, but it's now a staple in your life.

The learning curve may be a little higher, but they will get there as well. The bottom line is: The earlier the better.

When I talk about technology training, I am, for the most part, referring to the process of utilizing computer-based intervention known as CBI. This practice involves specialized software programs that have been developed for individuals with special needs to train in areas such as language, academics, social skills, and life skills.

I know that many of you are wondering how in the world you'll get your 3 or 4-year old child on the autism spectrum to sit still long enough to focus on computer training. Even a typical child has a hard time sitting still at that age, don't they?

After having used CBI for the past 13 years with individuals with autism of all ages, I can assure you that this methodology is extremely successful. There are reasons for this which I will explain in subsequent chapters. The important thing to remember, however, is the importance of starting early. In other words, start now.

In addition to CBI, I will be discussing the usage of other types of technology that should be incorporated into the lives of every child on the spectrum. These tools are used for many purposes: communication, organization, leisure, socialization, etc. Again, the sooner that these applications are introduced into the life of your child or the children you work with, the more you can be assured that these children will embrace the technological advantages that our society has to offer them.

EVERYONE NEEDS TO FEEL USEFUL

Recently, I collected data for a housing and lifestyle survey that involved questioning families who had adult children with autism or a related disability. The responses indicated that most adults with developmental disabilities are not involved in daily activities that the parents consider to be productive. Most adults still live at home with their families, while others live in a group home environment. Common activities include watching television, playing games, going to the mall, or going to the movies.

Some individuals are employed in the community, but this small percentage works at supermarkets or in drugstores bagging merchandise or stocking shelves. Several of them use the computer for browsing the Internet or playing computer games, but none of them use technology as a means of increasing productivity.

What this survey taught me is that it isn't enough just to get students to become technology-savvy. That's just half the story. The other half involves taking these skills and moving them into a functional role. I don't want to mitigate the importance of web browsing and game playing. These skills are important and essential to the lives of these individuals. But I feel that we need to take this skill set further down the road.

Everyone needs to feel that they're important in the universe. In my many observations of individuals with developmental disabilities, nothing is more essential to their fulfillment than knowing that they're performing a task that makes a contribution to their family, school class, group home, community, or simply their own lives. In other words, if the individual feels that he or she is helping or contributing in an important way to the group effort, the level of life satisfaction increases tremendously.

This concept is important to me for many reasons. I take it very personally. I have a mission in life to bring what I have learned and experienced to the lives of those touched by autism. I truly believe that every individual can learn to feel important and needed. It just takes the right kind of training and understanding for them to reach that goal.

Chapter One: Think Questions and Activities:

1. On a piece of paper, list two problems that involve adults with autism that you have been made aware of in your community. If you don't know, take a moment to ask someone you know who works with older individuals with autism or is the parent of an adolescent or adult with autism.

2. Write down three technological applications that you are presently using. Next to each one, jot down how this innovation helps you to be more effective in your life. If you have a child with autism, reread the story about Rachel, substituting your child's name in place of Rachel's. How do you feel when you imagine your child living independently and productively?

Chapter Two:

Following the Path Wherever it May Lead

"Accept the things to which fate binds you, and love the people with whom fate brings you together, but do so with all your heart."
-Marcus Aurelius

If you want to believe in fate, an autobiography of my life would prove your point. The fact that I became a speech pathologist still has my parents scratching their heads. My mother, an American by choice, raised her children to believe that speaking English well was of utmost importance. She was born in Frankfurt, Germany and suffered at the hands of the Nazis. After migrating to the United States in her early adolescence, she spent the first several years of her life in America trying to perfect the English language to the point that her nation of origin would be undetectable. Americans, she said, were not in love with Germans at that point in history, and the last thing that this young immigrant girl needed was more ostracism.

My mother did a great job. Most people would be hard pressed to identify any trace of an accent. The one issue for her, however, was the use of idioms, which she tried to incorporate into her daily language in order to sound as "American" as possible. To this day, I still have some trouble with them because I originally heard them from my mother a little backwards.

The real issue, though, was me. My parents said that I constantly garbled my speech when I was growing up, almost to the point of unintelligibility. I still remember being told, "You don't say words like banana or cabana (a very useful word in Florida) with the second "a" sound coming though your nose. Instead, the "a" should have more of an open-mouth quality." I think my muddled speech was a result of the fact that I was rather introverted and not especially secure as a young child. I had a tendency to keep my mouth closed more than open during conversation, which not only affected the ability of others to understand me, but probably contributed to those nasal sounding a's. The combination drove my mother crazy.

So, the day I called my parents from the University of Florida to tell them that I had changed my major from French (what was I thinking?) to speech pathology is a day my parents will never forget. How could a person who spoke so poorly as a child pick a profession in which the goal is to train others to speak well? In all fairness to the story, I must confess that in my senior year of high school, I discovered drama class. This training improved my self-confidence significantly and, in turn, my speech. Still, it was a very long stretch from the young girl who garbled her speech.

Eventually, I realized that a career as a French teacher no longer interested me, so I discovered that speech pathology classes were offered in the same department as my drama classes. My father was a physician, and I spent a great deal of time in high school volunteering at the local hospital, as well as working in my father's office over the summer. I enjoyed being a giver and a helper, so I was drawn to a therapy-based profession. I took the introductory speech pathology class, and I immediately realized that I had found my home. It was soon after that I made that call to my parents. So began the first chapter in this twist of fate.

Back in the day, it was common for women to follow their men wherever they would lead, so as a young bride, I ended up graduating college from the University of Miami because my husband had taken a job in South Florida. Interestingly, this college is within walking distance of the home where my parents have lived since before my birth. When I first applied to colleges, my parents offered me a car if I would agree to stay in town, live at home, and go to UM. I was so anxious to go away that even when they added a summer trip to Europe in the mix, I refused the offer. But here I was, just two years later, attending this exact school. Of course, since I was married, I didn't live at home, but I still wondered why the car and European vacation were no longer on the table.

A Bachelor's degree in Speech Pathology didn't take me too far, so I continued on to grad school at UM. The only glitch was that the graduate school tuition at this university was steep. Though the college is called the University of Miami, it's indeed a private school, so the cost was basically out of reach for a young couple. My parents and grandmother offered some assistance, but basically, I was on my own. Luckily, I had good grades, so I applied for a grant in the department of gerontology. If I agreed to take five extra courses in the field of gerontology, they would pay for my graduate school education. Sounds too good to be true, right? I decided to get a head start on the extra curriculum that was required, so during the summer before grad school started, I completed (on my own dime) three out of the five required gerontology courses.

Then, literally two days before the first semester of graduate school, I received a call from my advisor. "We're sorry to inform you that the gerontology grants have been re-routed," I was told. The speech department was not going to get them that year. They would go instead to the school of nursing. So, here I was, two days before I was to start grad school with absolutely no idea how I was going to pay for my classes.

The next day, I received another phone call from my advisor: "Good news! We found another grant for you. The University of Miami Medical School is offering to pay for two semesters of graduate school tuition and a $50-per week stipend if you agree to work Monday through Friday, 9AM to 5PM at their internationally renowned facility for the developmentally delayed population called The Mailman Center for Child Development." I began to contemplate what this new experience would entail. From a specialty in gerontology to an internship at a world famous center for children with developmental delays ... wow, that was a switch! And working 9-5 would mean that I would have to attend classes every night until 10PM. But, hey, it was the only offer on the table, and I grabbed it before they could say "tuition due tomorrow."

The Mailman Center for Child Development is part of the University of Miami School of Medicine's Department of Pediatrics. It was built in 1966 with funds from the Abraham and Joseph Mailman Foundation, the Joseph P. Kennedy Foundation, and federally funded grants. Its mission is to provide research, training, and services to children with special needs. In 1977, the year I spent there as an intern, the population of children included those with a wide range of disabilities such as spina bifida, untreated phenylketonuria (PKU), cerebral palsy, Down's Syndrome, developmental delay, and, of course, autism. For the most part, the children were under the age of five, and they came from all over the world.

The Center is also involved in many research studies. One of the most important aspects of this facility is that it uses an interdisciplinary team approach. This means that I worked alongside professionals from many different disciplines throughout my entire term. Needless to say, the education and training that I received from this job could never have been duplicated anywhere else. I learned so much about children with developmental disabilities, working with others as a team player, research, and the list goes on and on. I placed in the 93% on my Board exam because many of the questions referred to information I had learned, not in the classroom, but in this setting. I have often said that I was blessed with needing financial assistance at that time of my life. Otherwise, I would have missed out on one of the most valuable—and fateful—experiences I've ever had.

The Mailman Center experience earned me the right to bill myself as a specialist in the field of developmental communication disorders, so I was hired right out of graduate school as the speech pathologist for the first special needs pre-school program in Dade County, Florida. I was also exposed in this setting to young children with mental retardation and autism. There weren't so many of them like there are today, but at that time, if they lived in Dade County, they were in my class.

There was one little girl with autism who was living in a foster home and was up for adoption. For many days and nights, I pondered the thought of adopting her. My husband was somewhat open to the idea, although I ultimately decided against it. It just wasn't the right time for us to take on that kind of responsibility. Perhaps the angels of fate had something else in store for me at a later time.

After three years in the public school system, I realized that public institutions and I were not a good match. The first year that I was in the system, I was given funds to purchase materials for the new program and a great big classroom in which to work. By the end of my third year, funding had been cut almost to nothing, and I was literally working in the school's book closet alongside the elementary school's other speech pathologist. My head was full of ideas, and my heart felt trapped in the mire of bureaucracy. So, in the fall of 1981, I realized it was time for me to strike out on my own.

With two fellow public school runaways, Dimensions Speech, Language and Learning Services was born. Our third partner dropped out the following year, but the two of us forged ahead. In 1991, we decided to split into two different businesses. I became the North office, and she ran Dimensions South.

For the next several years, I developed my practice to the point that I was quite busy. I worked at private schools in the morning and in my office after school. One of the private schools where I worked was a residential facility for individuals with autism. During those years, it was common for children with autism to be placed in this type of setting. The woman that ran the school was a well-known and outspoken educator in the field of autism. She was very passionate about the children. For the most part, I remember that the children were quite involved at this particular school.

My Sons

To fast forward the story, I divorced Husband #1, got married to Husband #2 two years later, and delivered by first son a year and a half after that. Hunter was, by all accounts, delayed in the acquisition of his motor and speech skills. He didn't walk until the age of 14 months, and by 18 months, he wasn't saying much either. He understood everything, but his expressive vocabulary included two-word approximations.

I used to say that Hunter was "slow to warm up." When my parents or his other grandparents came over to the house, he wouldn't run up to greet them. Instead, he slithered away from their hugs and ran into his room. My parents learned to adapt to his nervousness by not going up to him at all. They waited for him to acclimate to them. If left alone, he would eventually become comfortable and make contact with them during their visit.

Thankful for my professional skills, I began to work on remediating his language delay. Hunter made steady progress but was still behind others his age when he started pre-school at two years old.

He attended one of the schools where I worked, and it was certainly a strange experience to have the child with the lowest verbal skills in the pre-school class where I was the speech teacher. As often occurs with language-delayed children, Hunter's social skills were not as advanced as the others either. He was very shy around his peers and didn't initiate activities. Again, it's worthwhile to mention that his receptive language was never in question. He followed directions well and had a great sense of humor. I can still recall the great big belly laugh that he was well known for.

Hunter's language eventually improved so that by the age of four, he had caught up to the proper level for his age. I often referred to my son, Hunter, as "my most important student." Though he continued to demonstrate some other sensory issues such as sound sensitivities (which we treated successfully with Auditory Integration Training-AIT) and compulsive tendencies, I felt he was out of the woods. But a much larger job was unfolding before me just about the same time as I was finishing up with Hunter.

Born 21 months apart, my second child, Blake, seemed to develop quite the opposite of Hunter. He walked early and started verbalizing in advance as well. He was also extremely interactive. He loved to play baby games like peek-a-boo and engaged in activities with his older brother. Their father, an avid amateur videographer, seemed to capture every moment of their young years for posterity. In one sequence, when he was taping my interaction with Blake, I am heard to say something along the lines of, "Thank goodness Blake is speaking early. At least we won't have to go through what we went through with Hunter."

By the time Blake reached his 2nd birthday, however, all of his speech skills had not only come to a screeching halt, but had regressed to the point of non-existence. Demonstrating a totally different scenario from Hunter's expressive-only delay, Blake did not follow directions or appear to respond to verbal information. He was remote and distant and did not respond to his name. Videos of him at this age show a distinct difference from the Blake of just a few months before.

Again, my professional experience kicked in, and since he had a history of chronic ear infections (we put tubes in his ears when he as about one-year old), I decided to rule out hearing loss as the culprit. I took him to a well-known audiologist who told me that his hearing was fine, but he seemed to be developmentally delayed. My thought at this time was that his ear infections could have caused an auditory processing issue or that he had verbal apraxia. My mother mentioned that maybe he had autism. This was shocking because I didn't know that she knew much about the disorder. This was back in 1993 and way before autism had become an international buzz word. Though I had been working with children with autism for 15 years by then, there was no way that my mind could wrap itself around the concept that Blake had it. So, I told my mother that she didn't know what she was talking about and retreated back to my own version of the problem.

Meanwhile, I began to work with Blake. For awhile, I was still doing therapy with Hunter as well (remember, they are only 21 months apart), so I hung schedules in the house: Hunter-4:00-4:30, Blake-4:30-5:00, joint lesson, 5:00-5:30. Each day, I diligently brought my children into my home office for their therapy sessions. I was quite the professional as I donned the hat of a speech therapist rather than a mother during their training times.

Blake made steady progress, initially demonstrating improvements in the understanding of language. This initial progress only fueled the fire of my denial. With urging from his teacher, I made an appointment to take him to a developmental pediatrician I knew because we shared children in my caseload. But as the time for that visit loomed near, I vacillated in my conviction to take him. Nevertheless, I kept the appointment.

"So, Valerie," the doctor asked, "can you describe the behaviors that Blake is exhibiting that are troubling you?" I came prepared with my list of issues: not talking, not coming when he's called, walking on his toes, etc. "If this was one of the children that you worked with, what would you say was going on here?" the doctor asked me. I hesitated before answering. "I think Blake has a prominent auditory processing disorder in combination with verbal apraxia."

"Yes, you're right," the doctor responded. "And what would you say these diagnoses are part of in the larger sense?" I didn't answer. It just wasn't going to be me who said the word. "I believe Blake is autistic, Valerie," the doctor spoke up. He went on to describe autism for Blake's father, who really had absolutely no idea what he was talking about. He talked about the movie, *Rainman*, which really didn't help my husband find a reference point at all. After about a half hour, we left the doctor's office. The only recommendation he gave us was the name of a school where we might enroll Blake.

The date was July 9, 1993. I didn't realize it at the time, but that day would function as the turning point in my life and the day that my life's purpose would be etched in stone. It was the day everything that I had ever done professionally made sense: becoming a speech pathologist, losing the gerontology grant, receiving the Mailman Center training position, starting the first pre-school class in my county for developmentally delayed pre-schoolers, working at the autism school, and even the work that I had accomplished with my first child, Hunter. My fate was sealed: Autism would become my mantra, both professionally and personally from this day forward.

Facing the Truth

On the way home from the doctor's office, I went into operational mode. In my mind, there wasn't time to cry. There wasn't time to argue with my husband, who didn't really accept the diagnosis for at least another year. It was time to get rolling. So, Blake did have autism. Okay, I could deal with this. It wasn't something I was unfamiliar with. The school that the doctor recommended was run by a woman I knew very well. She also had a son with autism, and I had worked with him for many years. I didn't have time to allow any grass to grow under my feet, so I called her while we drove back home. It was really a little like an episode from *The Twilight Zone.*

Having a few connections in the field proved to be beneficial, however. We were able to cut through the bureaucratic red tape, and Blake was enrolled in the school within weeks.

It's very strange to have a child with a disorder in the area in which you are knowledgeable. At first, I tried to pretend that I was just a mother with a son with this diagnosis of autism. I attempted to take the speech pathologist part of me and push it to the back of my mind. To be honest, it's what Blake's teachers told me to do: Just sit back and listen to them. Be Blake's mom, not his therapist. That was their philosophy. It worked for about six months.

Then, I think the shock of it all began to wear off, and I came back from the dead. I started to really look at what Blake's educational program was all about. Certain things were just not making sense to me, such as the way that the school was teaching augmentative communication. The method that they used to teach picture communication was not only something that I didn't totally agree with, but it also wasn't working with Blake. To be honest, I wasn't seeing a lot of progress in general. So, I began to speak up. I also began to do a lot of research into alternative programs for those with autism.

My journey led me to discover a program in Massachusetts that claimed autism was curable. They didn't claim that they could cure *your* child necessarily, but that coming out of autism was possible. My husband loved the idea of the word "cure," so he was extremely supportive when I decided that we would take Blake there for their week-long home training program. During the course of the week, we were trained in a methodology that we were to incorporate in our own home. It involved learning how to join your child's world in order to bring your child back into yours. That's a very simplified description of their philosophies, of course.

In order to accomplish the goals of this program, we were to keep Blake in our home and not allow him to leave it for any reason other than an emergency. They felt that the stimuli from the outside world were too distracting to him. He needed to be in a calm and controlled environment in order for him to be able to absorb the teachings that he would be exposed to 10 hours a day 7 days a week. Eventually, when Blake's level of attending reached a certain level, he would be ready to leave the cocoon in order to be reintroduced to the rest of the universe.

When we returned from Massachusetts, we embarked on creating our own home program that mimicked the one we had seen at their center. We built a room in our home with special floors, lighting, and shelving. I hired a staff of 14 individuals who would implement the therapy 10 hours a day under my direction and supervision. One entire wall of the room was converted into a two-way mirror so that I could watch the sessions without Blake seeing me. Every Sunday, the entire staff would join me for a feedback and goal-planning session. Blake never left the house, not even for a doctor's appointment. House calls were reinvented during this period. I ran this program for a year and a half.

During this period of time, the program that I ran in my home allowed me to be both a mom and a professional. I was able to maintain the integrity of the program while continuing to utilize my knowledge of communication and language. Blake developed considerably in certain areas, though not as much in others. At the time, the program did not accept other methodologies to be infused into it. This has since changed.

After a year and a half, I decided I wanted to bring in other therapies and treatments, so I reduced the program to half-days. I also felt that Blake had reached a point in which he was ready to go out into the world, so I re-enrolled him in a half-day school program and allowed him to go out for recreational activities.

The name of the program in Massachusetts is The Son-Rise Program®. It is offered by the Autism Treatment Center of America and is housed at the Options Institute. I can honestly say that the time I spent at their facility, as well as the experience that I had running a home-based Son-Rise® Program was extremely valuable to both Blake and me. Blake was not cured of autism, but he gained a great deal during that period which I know was a direct result of the program.

Shortly thereafter, we decided to take our family on a long-awaited vacation. Naturally, we picked Disney World. For some reason, I have always been mesmerized by that place. Even to this day, as soon as my feet touch the ground of the parks, I feel like I'm in my element. I especially have that experience at the EPCOT Center. EPCOT stands for the Experimental Prototype Community of Tomorrow and is dedicated to international culture and technological innovation.

During this trip, we visited an exhibit at EPCOT called "The Home of Tomorrow." In this Jetsons-style mock-up house, I was privy to technology that in 1996 was quite spectacular. The one innovation that I will never forget was touchscreen technology. It had a significant impact on the way I would view these applications for individuals with developmental disabilities. Each room utilized a touchpad for the purpose of controlling aspects of the environment. Remember, this was 1996, and most people had never seen touchscreen applications. Each of these was designed to increase efficiency in the everyday tasks of life. Of course, some of the applications which were unbelievable then would be considered dated at this point. For example, I remember seeing a DVD player. Back then, we all had video recorders, and the concept of a small compact disk playing an entire movie seemed like a dream.

As I walked around the exhibit in amazement holding hands with my then five-year old autistic son, Blake, the proverbial light bulb went off in my head. I may be understating that a bit. It was more like a hammer hitting me over the head. Regardless of the intensity, I had an epiphany: If this was to be the home of tomorrow, it would be the kind of house that my son would be living in as an adult. Therefore, he needed to be able to utilize all of this technology which was designed to ease the performance of daily functions. And, of course, as I always do, I was thinking not just of my son but of all of the children with developmental disabilities that I worked with as a speech pathologist.

APPLYING TECHNOLOGY

As soon as I got back to work, I began to investigate the computer software that was on the market for individuals with special needs. I started with language-based programs since I was in the business of teaching these skills. I found a software company called Laureate Learning Systems (more about them in later chapters), which had a very impressive array of software in DOS format designed specifically for this purpose. I also discovered a program called Labeling Tutor, which was created by an engineer who had a son with autism. Through Laureate, I purchased a touchscreen window that was applied to the front of the monitor with Velcro. Now I was set up to begin training my first "victim"— my son, Blake!

Blake on the computer

I don't remember the exact timing, but what I do recall is that Blake picked up the initial skills within a very short period of time. And he loved working on the computer. Soon, I brought Computer-Based Intervention (CBI) into the office and had all of the children involved. It wasn't long until the kids were hooked, I was hooked, and the parents who saw the amazing progress that their children were making were also onboard.

Several months later, while attending an autism workshop, I struck up a conversation with a woman about my work with children on the autism spectrum using computer intervention. She asked me if I would be interested in writing an article, possibly a review of a particular software program, for the Autism Society of America's then bi-monthly publication called the ADVOCATE. I wrote this review and soon thereafter wrote many others that were published in this periodical, as well as others. My reputation on this subject led me to receive invitations to lecture and teach workshops around the country and overseas.

But assessing computer technology doesn't stop with just CBI. There are many more applications that are important for our population. One of the most important is the use of voice-output systems that assist individuals with limited verbal skills to communicate effectively. This use is part of the field of augmentative communication. We have high tech and low tech applications that we use with non- or low-verbal people. Low tech usually doesn't involve technological applications, while high tech is all about that. In a subsequent chapter, I will discuss augmentative communication in detail.

Every parent of a non-verbal child wants that child to communicate verbally. Therefore, the first type of communication training introduced is commonly verbal skill training. This is not a book about this subject, so I won't talk about this type of methodology. But if this type of training is not completely successful, and the child doesn't appear to be able to communicate all thoughts through verbal speech, parents and therapists might consider bringing augmentative or alternative communication methods into the mix. The definition of "augmentative communication" is not synonymous with the term "alternative communication," though I often hear people using them interchangeably. *Augmentative* means assisting or adding to, while *alternative* denotes substitution. So, a non-verbal person would use the same application as an alternative means of communication, while the low-verbal person would utilize the instrument as an augmentative method. The truth is that augmentative communication should be brought into the communication training of every child who has either low or non-verbal language abilities at the very beginning. Research has shown that it increases verbal language acquisition.

The moment when parents recognize that it's imperative to include other communication systems in their child's life varies from person to person. I have had parents come to me when their child is very young, although this is not the norm. Usually, it doesn't occur to parents until the child is around age four or even six or older. It has only been through experience that I have learned how important it is to utilize augmentative methodologies early. The Son-Rise® program was, at the time I began working with it, a verbal-only program.

By the age of four, I realized that while Blake was able to say certain words when he was shown a picture, he was unable to remember them without a picture. His pronunciation wasn't at all understandable to anyone other than myself and the team that worked with him in the home program. It wasn't surprising that he displayed signs of considerable frustration.

When Blake was first diagnosed, he spent six months at the aforementioned school. During that time, the teachers and therapists attempted to utilize a picture system with him, but it was unsuccessful. This picture system, called the Picture Exchange Communication System (otherwise known as PECS), used black and white stick-figurish symbols to represent different items. Blake just didn't make the connection. I recalled that experience when I started to think about what I needed to do to increase Blake's communication abilities.

Looking around his room, I noticed that Blake had a large amount of toys that he often tried to request. I thought that he might understand the picture-symbol relationship if the picture looked more like the item it represented. As this was before digital photography, I began to design picture cards that looked like Blake's objects. Items such as simple foods weren't difficult because I could find well-designed clip art. Other things like Blake's puzzles involved designing cards that sometimes had up to 25 different pieces of clip art on them. This realistic pictorial system made all the difference in the world. Blake learned to communicate his wants and needs quickly and successfully.

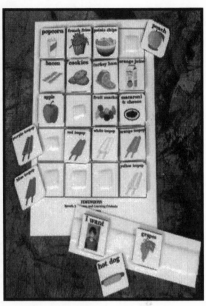

Blake using PECS   *Our version of PECS*

Of course, I then began to design cards for many of the children I worked with, as well as children with autism whose families I had begun to communicate with via the Internet. Word of my type of pictures eventually made its way to Frost and Bundy, the creators of the PECS program. While attending their advanced workshop, they made an announcement at the seminar that referenced my pictures. I can honestly say that after 30 years in the field of autism, PECS is truly one of the most important tools that has been created for non- or low verbal individuals. As you will find out in the subsequent chapters, PECS usage is often the first step toward utilizing a higher tech device. These days, we often use digital images in order to create pictures for this system.

| Banana | Strawberry | Pear |

It was during this time that I started implementing CBI with Blake and others, so my technology radar was turned on. Blake was doing very well with the PECS program, but by the time he was six, I began to notice that he needed to move on, as his abilities had surpassed the capabilities of the system. I began to investigate the devices that were available for this type of application. I noticed that some were on the cheaper end, and some were really quite expensive—in the thousands of dollars.

The ones on the less expensive end of the spectrum appeared to be machines that had a grid of anywhere from one to sixteen pictures on the front touchscreen. The child would be instructed to select the picture that represented the item he or she wanted. The machine would say the word selected. If the child wanted to select other items, they were only available if someone changed the settings on the device and/ or changed out acetates of the pictures. Usually, the voice on the machine was a recorded voice.

The more expensive equipment had something called a dynamic screen. This application had the capability of changing out the entire set of pictures just by pressing a button. Also, each button could be programmed with a pictorial representation that was available through the device's large vocabulary.

I contacted the school system's Assistive Technology department. The director of that program recommended the cheapest device for Blake. I wasn't surprised, but it didn't mean that I was just going to accept that advice. No, I had picked out a different machine. The difference in price was a mere $6,500. That didn't deter me from pushing for the one that I knew Blake needed, however. The director was quite upset that she had a mother on her hands who knew a little something, and of course, she challenged my decision.

The expensive device had the dynamic screen capabilities which I recognized would be the way that Blake would be able to communicate rapidly and effectively. The cheaper one would require someone to constantly change the levels of pictures for him. He was already communicating over 200 words with his PECS system, so having a device which limited him to a selection of only 16 pictures at a time would be more limiting than his current situation.

The director told me that in her opinion, Blake was not capable of using the dynamic screen device. Since I disagreed, however, she would give Blake a loaner device for two weeks. If he could prove his ability by that time, the machine would be ordered for him. If not, then it would be the cheaper one. Okay—deal!

When he received the loaner device, no one at this school had any idea how it worked, so the job of training him was left up to me. I didn't know how it worked either, so there was a learning curve for me as well. To add insult to injury, the device was not working for the first week of Blake's trial period. Unwilling to extend the time, the director gave us just one week to whip Blake into shape. She really didn't know who she was dealing with, though. Between myself, Blake, and some higher power, Blake not only learned how to use the thing, he soared with it.

Within one week, Blake demonstrated his ability to correctly select the item he wanted and change out pages independently. Needless to say, the school system ordered him a device of his own.

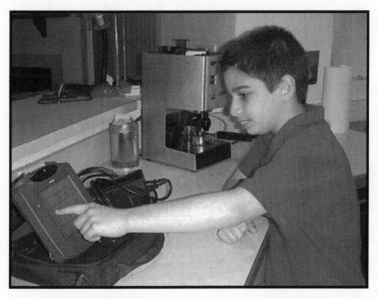

Blake using his dedicated voice output system

I realize now that the key to Blake's success was the fact that he had been involved with Computer-Based Intervention for quite some time. He was used to utilizing a touchscreen, as well as technology in general. Other factors that certainly contributed include the PECS training, which is another visual communication system, and the fact that people with autism are usually visual learners to begin with.

I guess I don't have to tell you that I brought this knowledge and experience with me to the office. I have been involved as an advocate for countless other children who were put into similar circumstances. I have not been a welcome face at the Individualized Education Plan (IEP) meetings for my clients. One assistive technology person actually threatened to take away Blake's device if I continued to pursue advocating for another child. Sometimes, loaners were not available for me to train my kids, so I used Blake's device. I'm just glad that I have been lucky in that my job places me on the side of the child, not on the side that must try to keep costs down. In Chapter Seven, I will go into more detail about augmentative devices.

In the next chapter, you will learn about other technological applications that are available. Technology has come a long way since I stood in the 1996 version of the "Home of Tomorrow." What seemed only a dream then has come true. Homes of today are able to be outfitted with many different types of high tech applications. And the "Home of Tomorrow" will be even more outstanding. My goal is to continue to increase Blake's level of sophistication with regard to technology. Of course, that goes for my students and all of the world's population of individuals with autism.

Chapter Two: Think Questions and Activities:

1. What experiences have you had in your life that can be used to help you parent your child with autism?

2. What types of communication systems has your child been exposed to? Which ones have been successful, and which ones have not?

3. Check out valerieherskowitz.com and sign up for our webinar on augmentative and alternative communication strategies.

CHAPTER THREE:

THE WORLD OF TODAY ... AND TOMORROW

"There is nothing like a dream to create the future."
-Victor Hugo

For Blake and many of the children that I have worked with, the real magic has been in the development of the touchscreen technology. Since touchscreen has so many applications these days, I decided to research how it works and where the technology began.

Believe it or not, the first touch surface was developed in 1974 by a company called Elographics (now called Elo TouchSystems.) They are responsible for the patent on the touch technology that we use today. It works similarly to a mouse, but utilizes a touch sensor, a controller card, and a software driver. The controller is a small PC card that connects between the touch sensor and the computer. It acts as the translator between the two parts. The driver makes the computer interpret the touch as if it were a mouse click, so you can use existing software. You can buy a touchscreen as an add-on to put over your existing monitor, or you can buy the new HP Touchsmart, which has the touchscreen built in. (We just got one for Blake, but the whole family loves it!)

For many people, the iPhone was an unbelievable invention, but Blake has had his touch communication device for more than 10 years. When I went to China to teach speech pathologists about computer-based intervention, I thought they would be impressed when I demonstrated touchscreen technology. They were very respectful, but they took me to dinner at a restaurant that night in which all of the ordering was done by the customer using a touchscreen. What was I thinking? Did I really think that I, as an American, had any new technology to bring the Chinese? Well, they weren't up to snuff on the use of computers for teaching speech, so I guess I did help them after all.

All of this research on technology whetted my appetite for more, so I decided to return to the place where my journey into the world of technology had begun. One day in April 2008, I returned, with Blake and my husband, to the "Home of Tomorrow" at EPCOT to see what had changed. But much to my surprise, the "Home of Tomorrow" no longer existed. They had built something in its place called the "Home of Innoventions."

I asked one of the hosts about the name change since all of the products on display are currently available in the marketplace. What I was about to preview was not something we had to look forward to in the future but could enjoy today.

Before I actually entered the mock home, a demonstration of the keyless access system was performed. This application by the Kwikset company, called SmartScan, allows individuals access through fingerprint reading. You can set the system to allow access to different people at different times. If you want the continuous ability to enter the house, your setting would be on "continuous." If you have someone working in your home, you would set their fingerprint to only allow them access during certain hours.

My mind quickly thought about how this system could be advantageous in the home of someone with disabilities. The system could allow a caretaker to come and go without having to be let in, and access could be restricted to the appropriate times. How great is that? This application could certainly increase the independence of a person with special needs.

There were so many cool things in this home. In the kitchen, the refrigerator (coolMedia by Siemens) had a 15" flat screen television built into it, as well as an antibacterial system.

All systems in the home were integrated through a system by AMX. This allows the resident (or caretaker) to have a remote control device to activate and set lighting, entertainment, cooling and heating, security, window shades, etc. through one central system. If you want to give your loved one more independence, you can actually pre-set these applications and be free of worry. You can set the system to turn lights on and off in different rooms at certain times. You can set the air or heat to come on at the appropriate time, and you can even control the entertainment through this system.

Speaking of entertainment, the system that was on display was from a company called OneVoice™ Technologies. This system allows you to walk in a room and use your voice to play music, watch TV, send e-mail, make a phone call, and more. Just by speaking, you can control many aspects of your home. This system would be great for our children who can speak but are unable to coordinate all of these functions using devices. Imagine entering a room and just saying, "Call Mom" or "turn on *Blues Clues.*" It works with photos, too, so you can just give your photo album a name and order it to come on. Instantly, your photos are displayed.

It works with Skype™ as well. With Skype™, you can make free calls from your computer. If someone else is on the Skype system (or you're calling a toll-free number), the call is free. If you call someone on a land line, there is a charge, but the best part is that it supports videoconferencing. If you have a webcam, and the person you're calling has a webcam, you can actually see the person you've called—for free! I use this service all the time to conduct consultations with my clients. I actually perform evaluations and consultations around the globe using this technology, but how fabulous would it be for an individual with developmental disabilities to be able to walk into their house and say, "Call Joe." Within seconds, Joe would appear on the screen. Your child could do this with you or with a caretaker. Wouldn't a system like that increase the independence of our children? And what I find so mind-boggling is that this technology is available today—right now.

Recently, I decided to put this technology into action in order to monitor Blake when he's at home. We tried an experiment: I downloaded Skype™ onto the computer in his room. Then, I placed a call to him from another room in the house. I explained to him how to answer the call and start the video component. From there, I commenced a room-to-room relationship with him via videoconferencing.

At first, Blake wasn't sure what to make of the situation. I started the process by giving him short one-step commands to see if he could understand that I could see him even though I wasn't actually in the room with him. After awhile, he got the hang of it, and since that time, we've been using the application to help him become more independent in our home.

Of course, there was even more to discover at the Home of Innoventions. I loved the bathroom. The shower was incredible (called the DTV Custom Shower Experience by Kohler Co.) Again, there were applications that can be pre-set, such as the temperature of the water and the length of time of the shower. This product would be wonderful for my son, Blake, because I always have to set up his shower or bath since he's unable to adjust the water temperature himself. I then have to monitor him, as he has a tendency to fool around with the faucets. With this system, I could pre-set the water temperature and stop worrying that he could get scalded, and this would allow him a great deal more independence during shower time. I could even determine the length of the shower so that I wouldn't have to monitor him.

The shower itself has many different jet settings. There are multiple shower heads available. Wouldn't that be terrific for some of our children? A real sensory experience. I know that many of the kids I work with love water and do well in a Jacuzzi. Imagine being able to take a shower where there are multiple jet streams to relax them.

The windows in the home were also very interesting. They didn't have any curtains or blinds to cover them. Instead, they incorporated a sensor that detected light, making them dark at night and clear during the day. Again, I thought about Blake. How often do I tell him to open all of the blinds in the house and close them again after sunset? I'll admit that he derives satisfaction from the job, but he still needs to be told to do it. If he were living in a home with light detectors built into the windows, it would be one more step toward increasing his independence. This application was created by Research Frontiers Inc. and is called SPD-Smart Glass.

THE "DREAM HOME OF INNOVENTIONS"

After my experience at EPCOT, I began to furtively research what else had been invented. I came across a project that was in process in—of all places—Disneyland in Anaheim. It seemed like my life was intrinsically connected with Disney. The project was slated to be finished in just one month. What I discovered was that a consortium of companies had been commissioned to build a 5,000-square-foot home. This home would not only include the highest technology available, but a space age design as well. This structure was beginning to make the mock-up home in EPCOT look "Mickey Mouse" (pun intended.) It was called the "Dream Home of

Innoventions." I knew that I had to see this structure, so I set out to make my *dream* come true.

My correspondences began with the CEO of the building company that designed the home, Taylor-Morrison. I told her that I was interested in seeing the home at Disneyland when it was finished. I mentioned that I was involved with a group of parents who were interested in building a community for adults with developmental disabilities and that I wanted to see if the Dream Home had features that could be incorporated into those homes. I also told her that innovative design and high end technology hold the key for these individuals to be able to live in the most independent way possible. I must have perked her interest because shortly thereafter, I received a call from their President for the Southeast United States. He said that he was very interested in meeting with my group and that Taylor-Morrison might be interested in participating in the project.

He then put me in touch with David Miller, who is Disneyland's Director of Alliance Development. Dave had been instrumental in the development of the Dream Home since its inception. The project was a collaborative effort between Disney, Microsoft, Hewlett Packard, LifeWare, and Siemens Corporation. Dave and I corresponded with each other for several months before the Grand Opening of the Dream Home in June of 2008. By mid-July, I was on a plane to Anaheim to tour the Home and meet with David.

My experience at the Disney project was fantastic. The Dream Home exceeded any expectations that I could have imagined. The design of the attraction was interactive in nature, which was different from the tour-through style of the EPCOT home. The attraction was designed to emulate how a real family would incorporate all of the high end technological applications, so they used actors, who represented family members, to demonstrate each item.

The first application that I noticed involved massive amounts of electronic picture frames displayed all over the house. The pictures were displayed much like the photos of family in my home, but each of these frames was electronic and controlled by the home integration system.

The integration system was by a different company than the one in the EPCOT home. In this project, they used a company called LifeWare. Again, the ecosystem of the home was entirely operated through the use of the touchscreen-friendly keypad or remote control. But they took it a lot farther: Not only could someone control the lighting, temperature, window shades, music, and security with the touch of a finger, but microchips could be integrated into an individual's clothing to activate the systems in the house. So, for example, if your son requires the temperature to be 75 degrees, and he likes to listen to music from his favorite Disney movie, this would all take place as soon as he walks into a room of the house.

You could even arrange to have photographs that he likes automatically projected on a screen in the room! Think how much better our kids respond when the environment is suited to their needs! By the way, I heard that Bill Gates has been using this technology in his own home for many years.

This application uses technology called RFID, which stands for Radio Frequency Identification Tags. These tags are specially coded pieces of cloth or plastic that use radio frequencies to transmit information.

Another application using RFID technology was demonstrated in the kitchen of the Dream Home. Each food product in the kitchen was equipped with a microchip. When a food is eaten, the system works like an ongoing inventory control device, keeping track of exactly how much remains. When you need to replace the product, it shows up on your electronic shopping list.

The center island of the kitchen was equipped with an embedded cookbook, which was voice-activated and incorporated voice output technology. So, when you're ready to cook, you just talk to your countertop—literally. The cookbook turns on and is illuminated within the countertop. You speak your selection, and it talks back to you, giving you the appropriate directions. If you put the ingredients on the countertop, the RFID chip figures out if you have enough of the products remaining for the recipe. If not, it can't help you there, but the item is added to your shopping list.

Since culinary arts is one of the vocational fields that many individuals with autism pursue, I found the kitchen technology to be an extremely important application. I fantasized my son, Blake, in his kitchen preparing some of his own meals using "Lucille," the talking cookbook. I thought about how he could then take his grocery list, prepared by RFID technology, to the store or, better yet, have the items automatically delivered to him.

You may think that RFID technology is something that won't be available to the general public until the distant future, but Wal-Mart already uses the technology and is requiring that all of its vendors supply RFID chips in their products shortly. Best Buy, Target, Tesco, and others will follow Wal-Mart's lead shortly.

Aside from retail applications, RFID technology is already utilized in healthcare, manufacturing, transportation, defense, and more. You're probably already using this technology without knowing it. Do you have a transponder for tolls or to enter a restricted area? Do you use a Speedpass when you buy gas at Exxon/Mobil? Perhaps you bought one of your kids a *Star Wars* toy that interfaced with a base station. These are all examples of ways that RFID technology is already being used.

Once RFID chips are embedded in most product packaging, the chip will not only help us with inventory control, but we will be able to instantaneously download information from the Internet about that product. For instance, you will automatically be able to see nutritional information about any item.

You may remember from a previous chapter that I talked about a bathroom mirror that was actually an informational device. At the Dream Home of Innoventions, this Magic Mirror technology was also on display. This is extremely new technology. Through the camera, it figures out who is looking in the mirror and offers several applications. Perhaps you want to try on different outfits. You can do it without ever putting on the actual garment as the mirror will display an image of the outfit with you in it!! Or it will recite your appointments for the day. In the case of individuals with autism, it could display their schedule for the day in visual format. Hello, independence!

You may have heard or seen the product called Microsoft Surface. At Disney, I had the opportunity to play around with one of these. The computer is embedded into a table, and the product provides interaction with digital material through hand gestures, touch, and objects, such as a camera. It's basically a PC with an acrylic frame on top of it. Through an integration of cameras, the user can interact with the surface by touching or dragging his or her fingers across the screen or placing tagged items on the top that can be read by the system. I was able to even read books on the Surface and play interactive games.

In certain AT&T stores where they have Microsoft Surface, clerks can drop a few telephones on the top of the product. Instantly, the specs of each phone are displayed, including coverage plans, price, and features.

After I finished my tour of the Home, Dave took me upstairs to visit the Honda Exhibit. This attraction was featuring ASIMO or **A**dvanced **S**tep in **I**nnovative **Mo**bility, the most incredible robot you have ever seen. It's so lifelike that it's a weird feeling to watch it. Designed to be an assistant to humans, it responds to voice commands, walks, talks, dances, helps with household tasks, and even runs. ASIMO has a camera in its head, so it can access the movement of objects and assess their distance and direction. ASIMO recognizes postures and gestures, so it can respond to waving or pointing. The robot assesses the environment and is able to recognize potential hazards to which it can alert the people in the home. ASIMO can even respond to names and face people when it is spoken to. It can nod or shake its head when asked a question, and last but not least, it can recognize up to ten different faces.

As I walked around the Dream Home, I was awestruck by how far technology had come since 1995 when I first visited the "Home of Tomorrow." I realized that touchscreen technology had impacted our world to the extent that my son had a greater potential to live in a more unrestrictive environment—just like I had imagined so many years ago.

Of course, applying these technologies to our children's lives has yet to be maximized, but the opportunity is there. It's an amazing experience to brainstorm how all of the technology could be utilized to our children's advantage. Though not all of the applications are available yet, they will be available within three to four years just when my son and so many others with autism will be coming into their own.

I already have the new HP Touchsmart Computer at home, which uses total touch technology with no additional hardware. I first tried this computer at the Dream Home.

Blake and His iPhone

Just last December, Blake all of a sudden took an interest in my iPhone. It was strange because he just picked it up and began to use the applications as if he had already been taught. Yet, he had never seen it before. He just immediately started using YouTube and the iPod application. This was the beginning of a whole new experience for him. By the time the holidays rolled around, he was hooked, and the family all chipped in and bought him his own touch iPod. With absolutely no training, Blake was able to navigate all around the thing. When you analyze the reason for this, it's apparent that his ability is due to the fact that the iPod looks just like his communication device.

They both use touch technology, have visual icons, and have dynamic screens, which means that a whole new screen lights up with just a touch. I guess Blake thought it was a new machine for him. (Who else?) That is just one example of how being exposed to technology at a young age translates to the development of these innate abilities in our children. And these abilities turn into functional skills later in life.

I have just one more little piece of technology to tell you about. It isn't anywhere in the realm of the stuff at Disney, but it's cute and functional. Every time I talk about it at a lecture, someone asks me to repeat the name. It's called the Oral-B Triumph. It's an electric toothbrush that incorporates something called Smart Technology. This oral hygiene device comes with a separate digital display which visually demonstrates which teeth you should be brushing. Every 30 seconds, it switches areas and prompts the user with a stutter in the motor. Supposedly, we are to brush each of our teeth for two minutes for proper oral hygiene. When the two minutes has passed (the screen also displays a digital timer), a happy face shows on the screen, and the motor stops. This device is a wonderful tool for our children. It is not only a great oral stimulator and cleaner, but it uses visual and kinesthetic cueing to help our kids brush their teeth correctly. I just love this brush. Watching the display has made Blake so much more tolerant of brushing.

I hope that by now, I have excited and enticed you enough that you see the importance of incorporating technology into your child's life. In the next chapter, I will discuss why I believe this technological journey can and will ultimately lead your child or student down the road to maximized independence.

Chapter Three: Think Questions and Activities:

1. Using the technology that has been described in this chapter, write down which ones you can imagine would be helpful to your child or students now or in the future.

2. Next to each application that you have selected, list two reasons why you feel that this particular innovation would be important for your child or students.

3. Look up the companies mentioned in this chapter on the Internet. How could these products make *your* life more efficient and productive?

CHAPTER FOUR:

COMPUTER-BASED INTERVENTION —
WHAT'S IT ALL ABOUT?

"Home is where you hang your @."
-Author Unknown

In the previous chapters, we talked about the importance of starting on the road to technology literacy early. But there is another reason why it's so important to start early, and this reason is based on the science and research that supports early training of any sort. It deals with early intervention and neuroplasticity, which revolves around the brain's ability to reorganize itself by forming new neural connections throughout life (Medicine.net). The brain is an organ that changes from response to experience.

There are several studies that support early intensive behavioral intervention (e.g., Anderson et. al. 1987, Fenske et. al. 1985, Lovaas 1987, Smith et. al. 2000). Though the types of therapy models have varied in the studies, they have certain things in common. They all incorporated curriculums in the areas of attention and focusing, language, and social skills, and they all used a behavioral approach. Each model utilized 25 hours per week of structured stimulation, and they promoted the inclusion of parents and families into the intervention process. When these factors occur together, there is evidence that many children show significant increases in communication, IQ, and educational placement.

Computer-Based Intervention or CBI incorporates all of the above features. There are software programs that teach skills in the areas of attention, language, and social interaction, and they are taught using effective behavioral methods. I don't recommend that CBI be implemented 25 hours a week, but I do feel that it needs to be an integral part of a home-based intervention program. And I highly recommend that family members become active in the process.

From a physiological perspective, let's look at the reasons why early intervention is successful in utilizing the concept of neuroplasticity. According to the website, Neuroscience for Kids, neuroplasticity consists of several different processes that occur throughout a person's life. There are certain periods of one's life, however, where plasticity occurs more frequently. During the first two years of life, the synaptic connections of each neuron increase until there are twice as many synaptic connections as in an adult's brain. As time continues, there is a degenerative process called pruning which continues until the cell dies. This pruning process can be affected by the activity of cell interaction, however. Therefore, cells that are activated are strengthened, and those that are not activated are pruned. The pruning process continues until approximately age 16, so as you can see, early stimulation has a huge impact on brain development.

From a cellular and molecular level, researchers have demonstrated how sensory, perceptual, and language functions are influenced by our experiences. They have surmised that the brain is most susceptible to modifications for language acquisition within the first six years of life. The brain still retains the ability to acquire language skills in a slower manner up until the age of 12. After that, there is a significant slowdown. It doesn't come to a complete halt by any means, but it may be more difficult to accomplish.

Jason's Success Story

Jason had been diagnosed with autism approximately a year before his mother brought him into my office for a consultation. He was 3-1/2 years old and had received speech therapy services through the state funded early intervention program. For six months, Jason's therapist focused on developing his speech skills, which were non-existent at the time. She also worked with Jason's mother to incorporate techniques in the home. After the six months, the early intervention services ended, and Jason had not made significant progress in his ability to communicate his wants and needs. Needless to say, he was becoming increasingly more frustrated.

In order to get what he wanted, he pulled his caretaker to the area where his desired item was located, and he sort of flipped the caretaker's arm up toward the item. If what he wanted wasn't in plain sight, it usually took several attempts before the caretaker (usually his mother) figured out what he wanted. Sometimes, the failed attempts resulted in huge outbursts from Jason. What worried his mother even more was the fact that Jason was becoming more and more remote as his inability to communicate increased.

I asked Jason's mother if he had been exposed to any other communication techniques such as picture systems, sign language, or electronic devices. His mother said that toward the end of the early intervention services, the therapist had started some sign language, but he hadn't caught on to it yet. I also asked whether he had been exposed to technology in any way. His mother revealed that Jason did like to randomly push the keys on the computer keyboard, but there hadn't been any attempts to formally teach him computer usage.

I spent some time working with Jason to see what he was able to do and what he seemed to be interested in. He didn't show any interest in verbal speech, and he wasn't able to repeat the sounds or words that I demonstrated. I also tried to get him to imitate some gross motor movements like touching his head or clapping his hands. He was unable to accomplish this successfully, which led me to believe that he wasn't ready for sign language training since it requires the ability to imitate motor movements. His attention was very short, and he had difficulty focusing on these tasks.

Using toys, I tried to determine if Jason had the ability to cause things to happen. This skill, which we call cause and effect, is very important. If a child doesn't understand that he has the ability to make something happen, he won't understand the point of using communication, which is a cause and effect activity. Jason was able to demonstrate his ability to control in a very rudimentary way. Though he hadn't been exposed to computers formally, I took him to the computer to see what kind of interest I could muster from him. His focusing wasn't great, but I was able to grab his interest when I used entertaining and lively introductory programs.

Jason began to work with us in the office and with his mother at home. We began training him to use the PECS system using photos and also introduced him to a program I designed called Pre-Sign™, which develops the prerequisite skills needed to learn sign language. To increase his cause and effect skills, we introduced Jason to a wonderful series of animated programs that are used for young children with special needs. In addition to increasing this skill, we were able to improve his attention and focusing. We also used other software for developing his understanding of language skills. These programs, again developed for those with beginning language skills, helped him to comprehend the meaning of words.

After six months, Jason was able to communicate his wants and needs using the PECS system. He had finished the Pre-Sign™ program, and we moved him into our sequel program, Sequenced Sign™. He was using the computer via a touchscreen very well at this point. His cause and effect and attention skills had increased so significantly on the computer that we decided it was time to begin work on verbal speech. Instead of using traditional verbal behavior methods, however, which try to stimulate speech by having the child imitate the therapist, we used a computer program which has voice recognition skills. The child is asked to repeat different sounds into a microphone, and that action causes an animated character to perform. This activity proved to be quite successful, resulting in Jason attempting verbal imitation.

Jason continued to make great strides from there. After one year, he was verbalizing while using the PECS pictures and signs. He was quite communicative, which caused his behavior to improve. Eventually, we moved out of PECS into a dedicated voice output system. His experience in computer usage proved to be a tremendous asset as he learned to use the touchscreen communication device with ease. Through the device and computer-based intervention, he learned how to string words together to make short sentences. Ultimately, we were able to discontinue the voice output system because Jason developed the ability to speak on his own.

By the time Jason was in the first grade, he had been included in regular education with supports. He continued with his computer-based intervention program, in which the areas of advanced language and social pragmatics were stressed. As the years progressed, reading skills programming, especially in the areas of comprehension, were included in his training.

Jason is now eleven years old and in middle school. Though he still has challenges, he's living a life that includes the prospects of going to college. What is possible for him is beyond anything his parents could have dreamed for him just eight years ago. Technology continues to have a huge influence on his life: He e-mails his friends regularly and loves his iPod. He now wants a cell phone, which his mom has been thinking about getting for him.

Jason is a huge success story. The early influence of computer-based intervention proved to be the catalyst that helped him to become quite productive in his life. Not all individuals reach this level of functioning, but many do increase their abilities significantly through early technology training.

HELPING OLDER CHILDREN AND ADULTS

What if your child or student is older? Is all hope lost? Certainly not! As previously mentioned, brain plasticity does not stop for the entire lifetime of a person. Dr Merzenich, the neuroscientist often referred to as the "father of neuroplasticity," has been involved in some interesting work regarding older individuals. He and his colleagues have recently created a computer-based program called Brain Fitness, which is designed to strengthen the brain in order to increase speech and agility. Dr Merzenich's early work involved the research design of a similar computer-based training program called Fast ForWord, which I will discuss in detail in the next chapter. This program was designed for children and adolescents who demonstrate significant language impairments.

Think about the last time you tried to learn a new skill. Perhaps you and your spouse decided to take dance lessons, you decided to try to learn a little Italian before your trip to Italy, or you needed to learn a new computer application at work. There may have been a little bit of a learning curve, but you probably were able to gain some skill in these areas. Granted, it wasn't easy, and you probably won't be on *Dancing With the Stars* in the near future. But I'm sure you were able to learn enough to add enjoyment to your life.

Taking on technology in later years is much the same way even for a person with developmental disabilities. I have a student that is actually my age. (If you have done the math, you may have figured out that I'm in my early 50's.) We started working together approximately seven years ago. Bobby lives with his brother, who referred Bobby to me. At the time, Bobby's language consisted of one to two-word sentences, and he was difficult to understand. He had no reading skills and was unable to tell time. He was high functioning in other areas and held a job in the food court at the local mall, but he had virtually no experience using computers or any other technological application.

Initially, I felt that Bobby should focus on developing his language skills. I wanted to increase his ability to produce longer sentences, so I introduced him to a program called Sentence Developer ™, which I created for the students in my office. It's a visual system designed to teach sentence structure. (I'll discuss this program in more detail later in the book as well.) From a technological prospective, it's fairly easy to use. Bobby was able to learn how to use a mouse very quickly, so the touchscreen wasn't necessary.

This program was Bobby's first introduction into the world of computers. Though the technological learning curve was short, the impact of these exercises on his language development was significant. This experience also gave him the confidence to move on to more sophisticated computer usage.

We moved on to programs designed to improve his speech production. These applications, which are a little bit more involved from a technological perspective, allowed Bobby to record his own voice. We also incorporated a reading program, as well as an application to teach Bobby some time-telling skills. Through the last few years, Bobby has become quite skilled in computer technology. Aside from the skills he has acquired through the training, he feels that he's part of the world that he lives in and feels pride in his accomplishments.

Bobby loves the fact that he is computer literate at this time of his life. His brother purchased the reading program, and Bobby enjoys practicing the exercises at home. Bobby's story shows that we are never too old to acquire computer or technology skills.

Had Bobby been given the opportunity to obtain computer training when he was young, would he have been more able to utilize technology than he is today? My experience tells me that the answer to this question is yes, but this type of instruction simply wasn't available to him until seven years ago. Still, what he has accomplished in that span of time is quite remarkable and compelling. So, if anyone ever tries to convince you of the old adage, "You can't teach an old dog new tricks," please disregard it as an untruth.

THE RESEARCH

When I began my journey into the world of computer-based intervention, I basically acquired the programs and got started. I didn't spend time researching to see if there were double-blind studies showing that the practice was scientifically-based. And I took some grief for it in the early years, especially when I was asked to train professionals at a local hospital therapy clinic. I was called in by the medical director to design a computer-based therapy program for them. After I completed their training, they started to utilize the programs and experienced a great deal of success.

About a year later, the same medical director asked me to do a presentation on computer therapy for his medical staff. Strangely, in the middle of my speech, this doctor started to grill me on the research that had been done to substantiate the use of this methodology. Since I wasn't prepared for this, I couldn't answer his questions. Obviously, I was embarrassed, as well as angry. Later that day, I told the medical director that I would no longer be associated with his hospital, though I continued to use him as my son's physician.

The reason I didn't have the research at my fingertips was because I hadn't looked for it. Clinicians in the healing arts are trained differently from doctors and scientists in terms of how we implement techniques. As you may know, this often presents issues between the two factions. Since I'm a clinician, my training taught me that while research can provide a great deal of insight into certain areas of treatment, it often doesn't tell the whole story. My education emphasized creativity when working with individuals. In graduate school, we were required to design our own materials and programs and received high marks for novel presentations. So, it really didn't occur to me to do the research to see if computer-based intervention had any merit. I just tried it, viewed the results which were positive, and carried on.

To be honest, I don't think there really was much research on the subject back then, but that experience in the hospital taught me a lesson. Now, I never present on the subject without some reference to research. Since computer-based intervention is now a recognized treatment method, studies have been conducted and continue to be established, which verify the fact that CBI is a great method for training. So, for those of you who are interested in the research, I have three studies to report that involve computer-based intervention with individuals on the autism spectrum.

In 2000, Moore and Calvart, two psychologists from Georgetown University, conducted a study to examine the effect that computer training had on the acquisition of vocabulary in young children with autism. They compared behavioral programming and computer-based intervention with regard to attention, motivation, and learned word skills. The software used was designed to parallel the behavioral program, though it added interesting sounds and movements. The results of this study revealed that the children were more focused and stimulated, and they learned more vocabulary during the computer training versus the behavioral program.

A pilot study which evaluated reading development was conducted in the United Kingdom in 2000 by Williams, Wright, Coughlan, and Callaghan. Studying children ages three to five year old for ten weeks, the researchers judged these individuals in two conditions: reading a book or learning through computer instruction. The information gained from this study demonstrated that all of the children spent more time during the computer learning condition than they did in the book learning environment. Five out of the eight children were able to identify at least three words. This paper concluded that children with autism spent more time and were more enthusiastic during reading activities when utilizing computer-based learning.

The last study I'll report on involves social skill training through CBI. Usually, when I discuss pragmatics and social skills in reference to computers, people are quite puzzled. Learning how to interact with other people isn't something that most people would think could be developed using this type of tool. Quite the contrary, however, social development can be greatly enhanced using this technology. Bernard-Opitz, Sriram, and Nakhoda-Sapuan hypothesized that even though children with autism show difficulty in problem-solving during a social interaction, they have positive results when using visual cues such as pictures and animation. Using computer programs that displayed animated problem scenes, the children were asked to provide solutions. In the beginning, the trainers explained the answers to the children, again incorporating animation. Later, the children were asked to solve the problems on their own. The children were able to provide several alternative solutions to the problems, so this study demonstrates that children with autism are able to learn problem-solving techniques using CBI.

Laureate Learning Systems was one of the first companies to design language development software for people with special needs. I have so much respect for the founders of Laureate that I will discuss the company in more detail in Chapter 6. However, I wanted to mention now that the programs they have created have emanated from research on language development, and this research forms the basis for their software formats. Additionally, Laureate uses behavioral research for the trial formats of their programs.

Basically, their work is centered on the work of linguist, philosopher, and political activist, Noam Chomsky, who pioneered theories of language in the mid-20th century. His original theories have been revamped as of late (he's still around.) These programs don't just focus on teaching vocabulary words, but also incorporate other important elements of sentence structure early in the language learning process. They emphasize the fact that social skills are learned though expressive language practice, although vocabulary and grammar are acquired through input activities.

WHY CBI IS SUCCESSFUL

I have identified several factors that CBI offers which explain its success with individuals on the autism spectrum.

Predictability. Every parent, teacher, or therapist of a child with autism will agree that, for the most part, our children have issues with new people, new foods, and new experiences—just about "new" anything. Conversely, they seem to handle familiar situations well. They thrive in a ritualistic environment and deteriorate when something is strange to them. Computer-based intervention offers a mode of treatment that can provide familiarity and predictability. Certainly, this isn't the case the first time the individual begins the process, but as time goes on, the training takes on a *sameness* even when the actual exercise changes. The program starts up the same each time, and/or the animation is the same. The format of the exercises is the same, and if you use multiple programs from a particular software manufacturer, the format of other programs is similar, if not identical, to the programs the child is already using.

As therapists, teachers, or parents, we will have a shorter learning curve as well since the software designers often create a series of programs that present different exercises in the same format.

Animation. I feel that animation is a make-it or break-it situation. Some children need the animation that is provided by many of these programs, and others find it a major distraction, may be afraid of it, or become over-stimulated by it. This is why many of the manufacturers of these programs have included the ability to turn the animation feature on or off. You don't have this ability, however, with off-the-shelf software or programs that you purchase in a store rather than from a vendor who sells software specifically for the special needs population.

The animation can be used for several purposes: First, it's used as a reinforcer, so that when the child performs the task correctly, an animated character comes out and congratulates the child for a job well done. Another function of the characters is as a prompt device. Often, they will appear above the correct answer when the child has demonstrated the need for cuing. Then, as the child progresses, the animation will not appear. Lastly, there are several programs that utilize animation as the actual characters in the program. In this case, the intention is to increase attention and focus on the task.

If you take a look at off-the-shelf software, you often find that animation is used for other purposes as well as the above. There may be several animations on the screen at a time, and this can be quite distracting to many of the kids. The last thing we need is for our children to be *more* distracted than they already are.

Looking forward instead of down. When I started working with children on the computer, there was one thing that I noticed immediately. It seemed that they had a much easier time focusing on what they saw on the computer versus what I presented on a table when I worked with them off the computer. I initially concluded that it was the computer program alone that caused them to be more focused and attentive. But after awhile, I began to realize that it was because they looked forward when working on a computer rather than down. When they looked straight ahead, I was able to maintain their attention for a much longer period of time.

I have done my own quasi-experiment and have often utilized this vertical plane presentation when working off the computer with the children as well. Sure enough, I have found that children do seem to be able to sustain attention more appropriately this way. It makes sense. It's more natural if you think about it. When you watch TV or talk to someone, what direction are your eyes looking? You may sometimes look slightly down or slightly up if you're talking to someone who is shorter or taller. But most often, we are looking forward. It's not only a better way to teach our kids, but it's also more pragmatically appropriate. Do we really want to teach our children to focus down? No, we want them to focus forward as they will need to do when conversing with another person or watching the teacher at school.

From a therapeutic and educational sense, it's important to always try to maximize learning for all students. One way that therapists and teachers accomplish this is by recognizing different learning styles in their students. Some obvious ones are auditory learners versus visual learners. Delving into the entire subject of various learning styles is beyond the scope of this book, but software manufacturers of these types of programs have taken into account that individuals will vary greatly in terms of which sense they learn from. Therefore, they have made considerable efforts to include a great deal of auditory and visual approaches. For example, pictures are one stimulus, as well as the voice of the narrator who gives the directive. The only time that this varies is when the task requires the individual to just respond to a visual *or* auditory directive. Then, of course, both the visual and the auditory are not given. We call this a multimodality approach.

The term "modalities" refers to the way information is processed. If it is processed by seeing the information, it's obviously visual. If it's processed by hearing the information, it's auditory. Even though every individual learns through one channel better than the other, in most cases, presenting information in both an auditory and visual format is the best way to maximize learning. So, the child sees the picture, hears the words, maybe sees the written words, and sometimes gets visual cuing, etc. This multi-stimulation is often how we can make sure that the student has had the best opportunity for learning.

So, are you ready to start the journey or at least ready to learn more about how CBI is utilized? That's where we will begin in the next chapter.

Chapter Four: Think Questions and Activities:

1. Think of a skill that you learned when you were quite young that is like second nature to you now.

2. Next, think of a skill that you learned at a later age that you can perform quite well.

3. Do you recognize when your child or student is comfortable in a learning situation? Do you feel that the "predictability element" helps him or her to focus? Conversely, can you think of a situation in which your child or student was not successful due to the fact that the situation was new and unpredictable?

CHAPTER FIVE:

COMPUTER-BASED INTERVENTION —
AREAS FOR TRAINING

"Training is everything. The peach was once a bitter almond; cauliflower is nothing but cabbage with a college education."

-Mark Twain

In this chapter, I will discuss the different areas included in CBI training. In the next chapter, I will delve into how to determine what specific skills in each area need work and how to pick the appropriate software to improve these skills.

The areas of training are:

4. Cause and Effect
5. Language
6. Attention and Focusing
7. Reading and Literacy
8. Math and Spelling
9. Social/Pragmatics
10. Speech
11. Life and Workskills

1. CAUSE AND EFFECT

In my experience, this first area is one of the most overlooked. This concept deals with non-existence. In other words, recognizing that an action causes a reaction. It's considered to be the first step in communication development. When we communicate, and I don't mean just verbally, we're trying to control our universe. Communication is how we make our intentions understood. This communication includes body language, gestures, augmentative communication, and even a smile or cry, which are all signs of intent.

Cause and effect begins to develop in a very young infant at around 4-9 months. Even at this young age, children begin to learn how to signal their caregivers though eye contact or body language in order to communicate their desires. Between 12-16 months, the body language usually turns into single words.

In young children with autism, however, this understanding of how the universe works often fails to develop in the typical manner. It's very common for me to see a child on the spectrum with no clue about how to gain control of his or her life. When we use the old terminology that children with autism are somehow "locked" in their own worlds, it's generally the lack of cause and effect that we're referring to. With no ability to interact with the people around them, they often do withdraw into themselves. As they get a little older, parents, and caretakers just take control. The adults give the child meals and other foods using clues that they have picked up from the child. As time goes on, the child may not appear to have any motivations other than a few obsessive needs.

Just the other day, I engaged in a consultation with the family of a three-year old child with autism. The child appeared to have a great deal of intelligence, evidenced by the fact that he was able to verbally read several words, knew all of his colors and shapes, recited the alphabet, and counted to ten. He was also able to repeat pretty much any word he was asked to say. The sad thing was that this child demonstrated almost no ability to communicate his intent. Occasionally, he pulled his parents into the kitchen to show that he wanted something to eat or drink, but that was about it.

So, when I asked his parents what he liked in terms of foods, activities, people, etc., they didn't have many answers. He *seemed* to enjoy his DVD's, but he never really signaled to anyone that he wanted to see them. He ate a few foods, but he never pointed at them or indicated that he wanted them. I explained to his parents that while he seemed to be a high functioning child in certain areas, he really was missing a key element of development that usually appears in infancy: cause and effect. And that is where I plan to start to work with this child. I need to establish his ability to let us know what he wants. We have to begin the process of getting him in touch with some things that "turn him on." Lucky for us, I have my secret weapon: the computer.

The programs that work on cause and effect are very motivating for most kids and can teach them how to really come out of themselves and learn how the universe works. Of course, CBI is just one tool used in this process, and other methods are beyond the scope of this book. However, CBI can be a very important aspect in the development of this essential skill.

Usually, we start very simply with cause and effect. We may even hook up a simple button-type switch to the computer to make it very easy for the child to respond. Even a very young or involved child can activate the computer in this way. The mouse, keyboard, or even the touchscreen may be too advanced for some children, so we use a device which looks like a big round saucer-shaped button. All that a child needs to do is hit the button, and it activates the computer.

2. LANGUAGE

After we have established cause and effect, we begin the process of training the child to understand language. As

I mentioned earlier in this chapter, the vocabulary and grammar of language is learned through the teaching of receptive language skills or language processing, which we do both on and off of the computer. The computer programs that we use for developing receptive language offer two modes of presentation: first, they offer the exposure aspect. They allow children to explore words by clicking or touching, followed by listening. During this part of the training, the child is able to see pictures and hear the names of the pictures. Through this exploration process, we develop the child's awareness of language. Most young children with autism don't focus and listen to what others say. Often, they're not interested in verbal language and appear to ignore us when we speak. Our words just don't seem to hold any interest for them. The specialized computer programs, however, use a lot of bells and whistles to attract the child's attention to the pictures, as well as to the verbal presentation. While we have other more specific programs that are used to develop attention and focusing, these language-based programs are designed to increase the child's interest and responsiveness to verbal communication.

The second mode presented in these programs is the recognition or identification aspect. The program presents tasks that ask the child to click or touch items in response to a question (for example, "where is the dog?") or to a command ("show me the dog.") This really begins the interaction process. The child is now starting to follow verbal directions and perform an action in response to verbal language. As the child experiences different programs, the information presented becomes more complex and challenging.

The receptive language programs themselves follow a particular order that is commensurate with the normal language developmental path. This is the real beauty of the system. There are other individuals who have taken the time to do the research with regard to how people learn language, and they have developed their software to parallel these milestones. As the end users, we just need to determine where in the continuum a particular individual should get started. Obviously, not everyone starts from the beginning. In the next chapter, I will describe a method to help you figure out where your child or student should begin.

Wherever the child should start, it's through the work of receptive language learning that the child begins to blossom. We usually see the child's world open up as a result of these programs. Their awareness of people and events around them begins to unfold. Over time, they become more plugged into those around them, and they begin to demonstrate abilities that let us know they understand verbal language.

As the children learn to comprehend all of the intricacies of language, we must also provide opportunities for them to express themselves as well. Therefore, we have also programs that encourage language expression. When we discuss expressive language, we do so in a global sense. In other words, we include verbal language, of course, but also other systems of communication such as sign language and picture communication, either with simple pictures or with a special device. These are the augmentative communication systems that were discussed in Chapter 2.

The cool thing about the software is that there are programs that help to develop expressive language no matter which system we use. Obviously, we want to expose all children to the verbal programs. In addition, children who are expected to benefit from augmentative communication training can use software that incorporates these systems successfully.

There aren't as many expressive language programs on the market as I needed, so several years ago, I developed a program called Sentence Developer ™. Initially, I created it as a hands-on kit but later adapted it for the computer. Basically, it's a set of exercises that break down sentences into their individual components using a picture-prompting method. Until recently, I offered it only to the children that I worked with in my center. I have just licensed it, however, so that it is now available to others as well. (See the back of the book for more information.)

Though language programs are usually initiated after cause and effect has been established, sometimes we do start the early phase of the receptive language training during the cause and effect instruction period. The way the language programs are structured, they also promote cause and effect, although on a higher level.

3. Attention and Focusing

As I have discussed, all computer-based intervention software will increase an individual's attention abilities, but there are certain programs that are specifically designed for the purpose of developing focusing abilities.

I have never met anyone with autism who didn't need to work on increasing attention abilities. The reason for this is that autism includes some form of attention deficit. For some, it also includes hyperactivity, but not for all. Each and every individual will need to spend some time boosting these skills. Therefore, I always recommend that CBI include some time specifically devoted to focusing and attention work.

When I speak to parents about a child's attention, they frequently tell me that their child has "great" focusing abilities. "How's that?" I ask. They then proceed to tell me that when their child is involved in a particular activity such as watching videos, playing Nintendo®, or putting together a familiar puzzle, the child can stay focused for a very long time: sometimes *hours*. In fact, they have a very hard time getting their child to disengage from the activity when they want their child to do something else. This situation is called *hyperfocusing*. It's a very common scenario for individuals who have some type of attention issue. They're able to stay overly focused on their desired activity and actually tune out the rest of the world.

When they're required to move on to something else, however, they have a problem that we call "shifting of attention." In other words, taking their intense attention off of what they are presently involved with and moving it to another activity. It's very common that individuals with autism display this tendency. We use words like *transitioning* to discuss the problems inherent in this situation. The same parents who tell me that their child hyperfocuses also will tell me that the child's attention to other tasks is poor. Some of the software that has been developed for emphasizing attention and focusing skills works on this concept of shifting of attention.

By the way, hyperfocusing isn't always a bad thing. Sometimes, that skill can come in very handy. For instance, my husband, who definitely hyperfocuses, has risen to the top of his field partly due to his ability to focus so intently on a job that the margin of error is completely eliminated. Also, his son, who inherited that quality, has always been a star no matter the job setting. His bosses have recognized that when they need someone to get the job done fast and efficiently, Seth is the one they pick. Because he is such a focused worker, he has been promoted several times in just the few years he has been in the working world. Both of these individuals, though not formally diagnosed, appear to have some form of ADD or ADHD. The characteristic of hyperfocusing that is prevalent among individuals with this diagnosis has become an asset to them rather than a problem.

That sounds nice, and you may think that there's no need to deal with hyperfocusing. But the truth is that shifting of attention is a much needed skill as well. Imagine that my husband is working on a job, but when his boss asks him to come into the boss's office, my husband either: (a) tells the boss that he can't come, or (b) ignores the boss entirely. These options simply aren't available. So, what a person with attention issues must learn to do is stop hyperfocusing, handle the other task, and return to the first task, if needed. It's very difficult for these people, I assure you. That's one of the reasons why our kids have such a hard time with attention and focusing.

The time that is spent on improving attention and shifting of attention can also be considered to be the "brain warm-up" period. Much like the warm-ups we do before exercising, the brain can be subjected to a similar experience by doing tasks that require the person to focus. This is actually a good thing for anyone who is about to embark upon a mentally challenging task.

So, I commonly recommend that the individuals I work with start the CBI session with a short round of attention and focusing exercises. How long we do these really depends on the student. A good rule of thumb is to do the warm-ups for approximately five minutes for each half hour of CBI. So, if you're able to work with your child or student for a half hour, five minutes of these exercises is fine. Do ten minutes for CBI sessions that last an hour. Conversely, if your student is only able to do CBI for 15 minutes, 2-3 minutes of attention and focusing exercises is adequate.

4. Reading and Literacy

The latest research reveals that there is a lot going on between the language-literacy connection. Children with language issues often have difficulty connecting ideas or making inferences. This presents a big problem, as much of the literature today requires the reader to make inferences. Therefore, our kids often struggle when it comes to reading and literacy.

Jonathon is a good example of this issue. He was extremely delayed in acquiring language skills, but he did learn to speak fairly well. When the time came for Jonathon to learn to read, he displayed a great deal of difficulty, especially in the areas of reading comprehension. He was able to read a short passage and answer several of the multiple choice "wh" questions which had a definitive answer that he could find in the reading passage. The problem started when Jonathon was asked to figure out the underlying meaning (inferencing or problem-solving.) He could tell what color bathing suit the boy in the story was wearing at the beach on the hot and sunny day because it was directly stated in the story. But when asked what season it was, Jonathon had a hard time figuring that one out. It wasn't written in the story. Instead, Jonathon needed to figure out that if the boy in the story was at the beach on a hot and sunny day, then it was probably summer, late spring, or early fall. When he was given the choices of winter or summer, however, he hadn't a clue. This is what is meant by "inferencing"—figuring out what is going on from the information stated in the reading passage even though the answer is not directly stated. There are software programs on the market today that work directly to teach these abstract reasoning skills.

There are also other reading-based programs that are designed to teach phonics. Sometimes, children with autism struggle in this skill set. There are some children who just cannot learn phonics, however. Program after program has been attempted, and all that remains is one very frustrated child, along with a frustrated teacher and/or parent in tow. For these individuals, there are programs that bypass phonics altogether. They use a word recognition approach, which is often extremely successful. I have had the opportunity to teach countless numbers of children how to read without ever teaching the rules of phonics to them.

5. Math and Spelling

From an academic perspective, spelling and math skills development programs using visual prompt methodologies are available. Most of our children are visual learners, and these programs use this strength to teach these important abilities.

You may remember when teachers utilized counters or even an abacus. These tools use visual aids to assist in explaining number concepts to young individuals. For our children, using visual representations is essential. The software that is on the market is designed to provide this assistance to individuals with special needs. In order to maximize the visual modality to teach spelling skills, these programs use a combination of visual memory tasks and fill-in-the-blank with the missing letter exercises. This approach allows for children with poorer auditory processing skills to acquire better spelling abilities.

6. Social/Pragmatics

This may come as a surprise, but we spend a great deal of time training social skills through CBI. Research has indicated that social skill impairment is a common issue among individuals with ASD. [1] It is not that your child isn't interested in his or her peers, but he or she simply lacks the necessary skills to have these interactions.

You may not think that social skills can be taught through the computer, but social skills training can improve interactions, teach the steps needed for appropriate social situations, help children navigate through tough school situations, and increase awareness of emotions, just to name a few. In my office, I often see children who really don't know that they're supposed to do during everyday interactions. As a result, they may shy away from others or unknowingly act in an

1 Jennifer Jacobs, Development of Social Skills in Children with Autism Spectrum Disorder (ASD)

inappropriate way. The social skills tasks that are presented in these programs can teach them how to handle situations like these. After these skills are mastered, they can be practiced in real life settings, making the skills functional.

7. SPEECH

I'm a speech pathologist, so I can't leave out software for speech development and improvement, though I don't use them very often with children with autism, at least not until they become more verbal. Some kids are lucky and develop good pronunciation when they start to speak. Others do not and need a great deal of training with certain sounds or particular sound patterns.

Some children have a condition called *verbal apraxia*. This diagnosis means that the child's brain doesn't tell the mouth how to formulate the movements in order to make particular sounds for speech. In its most severe form, a person is pretty much non-verbal. There may be a few sounds that the child makes, but not many. Speech training shouldn't be abandoned in its entirety in a case like this, but if a child exhibits this level of severity, the training should focus on establishing other forms of communication as the primary goal.

There are less severe forms of verbal apraxia which we call *dyspraxia*. (**A**praxia means the absence of speech, and **dys**praxia means a dysfunction of speech.) For the individuals with some verbal language, the speech programs offer great opportunities for pronunciation training.

In addition to the praxic components of speech, individuals with autism may display articulation and phonological processing issues, which can result in the need for pronunciation training. Articulation errors are categorized sound substitutions, omissions, or distortions. For instance, if your child always pronounces the sound "th" as an "f" (i.e., the word "thumb" is pronounced "fumb"), that would be an articulation error. There are other common mispronunciations such as the "w" sound substituted for the "r" sound, so that "ring" becomes "wing." Another common one is the "w" sound substituted for the "l" sound, so that "lamb" becomes "wamb." There is also, of course, the infamous lisp, in which a person sticks out the tongue and makes a "th" sound where an "s" should go. These are just a few examples of many possible articulation errors. In general, these articulation errors are fairly easy to correct even in children with autism.

However, as a speech pathologist, I have to recommend that before you embark on a CBI program that includes articulation correction training, you should have your child receive an evaluation and some speech therapy training by a speech pathologist either privately or in the school setting. Then, you can use the software programs for reinforcement activities.

Similar to articulation errors, we have a category of sound issues that we call phonological processing disorders. These issues differ from articulation disorders in that they affect patterns of pronunciation, not individual sounds. For instance, a common phonological processing disorder is when a child leaves off the last consonant in the word (final consonant deletion), such as "cup" being pronounced "cu" with the "p" omitted. Other common phonological processing patterns include *cluster reduction* when one of the sounds from a blend of letters is omitted, such as the word "spot" becoming "pot." One other common process issue is called *fronting*. In fronting, the child's tongue comes to the front of the mouth instead of articulating the sound properly in the back of the throat. This causes words that have back sounds like "k" and "g" to sound like "t" or "d."

Children with autism often display issues with phonological processing as a result of the fact that they have auditory processing difficulties. These problems can cause not just pronunciation issues, but may also present phonological awareness complications which lead to reading problems. Because auditory processing affects the information that we need to learn both speech and phonics, I highly recommend that every one of our children devote time to phonological awareness within their CBI programs. Like attention and focusing, bigger gains can be made in the future when a certain amount of time during each CBI session is spent on developing the prerequisite skills for reading and speech. It's important to build these foundation abilities early on.

8. LIFE AND WORKSKILLS

There are quite a few programs available that help teach life skills. Included are programs that reinforce the steps for personal hygiene and dressing. In addition, there are visually-based programs to teach them how to tell time and how to recognize community signs, as well as shopping skills, including money concepts. I also include software for training basic math skills in this area. From a functional perspective, math skills, of course, are quite important.

The workskills programs teach data entry skills and order processing abilities. Paired with regular word processing programs, many of these individuals are quite capable of learning computer-based skills that can help them later on when they enter the working world.

Chapter Five: Think Questions and Activities:

1. Can you think of a situation in which your child hyperfocuses? In what ways is it an asset? When is it a hindrance?

2. Try a few brain warm-ups for yourself. When you get up in the morning or when you're on your way to work, see if you can do math timetables or some other brain warm-up skill. (Hint: I play Mahjong on the computer to warm up my brain.)

3. Make a list of the skill areas mentioned in this chapter in which you feel your child or student could use training.

Chapter Six:

Let's Get Started—Setting Up a Home CBI Program

"A Journey of a thousand miles, must begin with a single step."

-Lao Tzu

Initiating the CBI process takes a little planning. Four steps need to be completed before the training begins. When I work with families, I always go forward with these actions first before we actually start the programs.

Step One is an evaluation process that I call Prescriptive Software Selection™. The purpose of this course of action is to establish in what areas your child needs to train and at what level we need to start. The determination of the levels is especially important in the areas of language. Once these specifications are defined, we can proceed to Step Two, which is to select specific software that fits the areas and levels determined for your child.

The next two steps go hand in hand and are extremely important in making the CBI program successful. Step Three involves the funding of the program. You will find a Financial Planning Worksheet at the back of the book. It's imperative that you complete this process before beginning the actual CBI training. I feel that every training program, whether implemented in the home, school, or clinic, needs a financial plan. Too often, I have met families who have started something all gung ho only to run out of money somewhere in the middle of the process. Maybe you can relate to this. I wish I had a dollar for every family who has been down this road.

Unfortunately, I rarely meet a therapist, behaviorist, or physician who brings up this subject with their clients when creating their treatment plans. I always do. Since this is kind of unusual, my clients are often taken aback when I bring it up. You can imagine how surprised parents become when I say that I believe they're spending too much on my services! How many times has a doctor or professional told you that?

Well, there's a good reason why I do this. I believe that my job is to help not just the individual with the developmental issues, but also the family. How can I be helpful if I recommend a treatment plan that ends up causing a huge financial burden for the family? Isn't parenting a special needs child hard enough? I suppose being a parent to Blake gives me the perspective that part of my job is to put together a program in which we can get the biggest bang for the buck. The great thing about CBI is that it is an extremely economical intervention program. It isn't free, of course, so a budget needs to be created.

Many families ask what it will cost if they buy everything that they need. First of all, I don't know the answer to that question as CBI is an ongoing experience. You don't just purchase everything you need from the get-go, and then, you're done with it. Also, if I tell someone a particular amount and it's off the charts for them, they may feel that unless they can buy it all, the whole program is a big waste. And nothing could be further from the truth. Yes, there are minimums. If someone tells me that they only have $100, I can recommend one decent software, but buying one software isn't a CBI program.

So, instead of trying to go "shopping at the software mall," I like to work backwards. I start with asking the family to think about where the funding will come from. This involves some creativity. Of course, it always starts with what you can come up with on your own.

This past week, I worked with a family to set up a CBI home program. When we were trying to figure out how to put together their financial resources, I asked them what their child received for Christmas last year from their relatives and friends. Even before she answered, I could tell from the mother's face that the collection of toys her son received was nothing but a pile of useless items taking up space in their home. She listed these products one by one. It was obvious that each toy was either sitting in the closet or had been given away because her son never showed an interest in any of them. She preferred to discard them, re-gift them, or donate them to her church, as they only served as a constant reminder of her son's problems. At that point, I felt comfortable making my point: How about this holiday season, send an e-mail or letter to each one of your relatives asking them to forego the usual toys and instead either make a donation to your son's Home Program fund or purchase a few software products from a wish list that you provide them? If they choose the latter option, have them let you know which computer program they will be sending so you so that you can cross that one off of your list.

Obviously, the same tactic can be used for birthdays. I took this road myself for Blake's birthday three months ago. I was tired of the clothes that didn't fit and had to be returned to the store. I hate going to the mall and shop online for just about everything. So, I chose to set up the fund and asked our relatives and friends to make a donation to the fund. After his birthday, I sent each person a thank you note and mentioned what I had purchased with their monetary gift. It was very successful. I did the same thing this past holiday season, and that's how Blake got his $400 iPod Touch.

Another way to raise money for a CBI program is to have a fundraiser. I have found that this concept works very well, especially when the family is a member of a tightly knit community or religious group. My families have organized block parties, backyard BBQs, spaghetti suppers, and Mitzvah days (that's a Hebrew word for "giving.") I have noticed that the smaller the community, the more successful the experience usually will be. I don't exactly know why this phenomenon is true other than perhaps smaller groups are closer and tend to rally around each other when one of the families is in need. If you aren't the fundraiser type, perhaps a friend or church member could take on the responsibility of organizing the event for you.

Step Four involves setting up the CBI schedule. When I talk to parents about scheduling, I usually hear one of two comments: "I have plenty of time to work with my son" or "When am I ever going to fit in time for this? I don't have enough time to accomplish the responsibilities that I have now." Frankly, it really doesn't matter to me which one of those statements I hear. We set up a schedule for CBI anyway. And interestingly, I have found that the families that are extremely busy get just as much, if not more, accomplished.

I'm sure you've met plenty of people who have so much time on their hands that they don't seem to be very productive, while you stand in awe at some people who seem to "do it all." I'm an organizer by nature (I do professional organizing as well), so I will spend time putting a good schedule together. You will find the CBI Scheduler at the back of the book to help you. It has very specific directions on how to schedule time for CBI.

As both a professional organizer and a speech pathologist, I sometimes need to help families get organized in a general sense before they can add the CBI component into the mix. This service ranges anywhere from time management to space planning in their house. Obviously, if your home is cluttered, and you can't find a little niche for your child to work, you will need to get your home in better shape before you attempt to start this program.

In general, a well-organized home and life schedule works well for individuals with autism. I know that the apple doesn't fall far from the tree because I can't function well either when my space is cluttered or my life is chaotic. Those of us (and I include myself in this group) who have the need for structure and routine are so much more productive when the setting is right. So, to be a little redundant, you may need to spend some time getting your time and home in order.

When setting up the CBI schedule, we need to take several factors into account. First of all, we need to look at your existing open time slots given your other commitments. I always try to work with what I'm given, but sometimes, I have to help the parents restructure their priorities.

Yes, I know your other child's baseball practice is three times a week (I went through that with my eldest son), and your daughter's ballet recital is in two weeks. You don't have to remind me that Thanksgiving is in less than a month, and everyone counts on you to host the big feast. Certainly, we can't leave out the fact that your latest project is due at work in ten days. The list goes on and on, and establishing your priorities is indeed tough. It always seems that there are more responsibilities than one person can possibly handle. But you need to understand that you have a child with special needs.

In my workshop, *The Ten Principles for Parenting a Child with Special Needs*, I explain that your special child is the center of your universe—the sun, so to speak. This person needs you the most—more than your spouse, more than your other children, more than your boss, more than your customers, more than your sister, and more than your brother or parents. At least for the time being. It doesn't mean that you're to neglect the rest of the world. I realize that it's a tough balancing act; I do it every day of my life. And if you need help with this, I'm just a phone call away.

A home CBI program doesn't always mean that you're the only one who implements the lessons. You should use anyone you can who has the ability (and time) to motivate and direct your child. It may be your spouse, an older child, or a caretaker. Of course, those of you who have an existing home program will find that CBI will fit in beautifully. If you are doing ABA (Applied Behavioral Analysis) in your program, your behaviorist will be thrilled to see that many of the programs follow a discrete trial format. And don't leave out Grandma. Having worked with hundreds of parents, I know that children are often cared for by a grandmother or grandfather while their parents are at work. I know that I'm generalizing when I say this, but most of the grandparents I have worked with do a wonderful job when they're given certain educational tasks to perform. Though some people are harder than others to train, most have understood the behavioral concepts that are needed. Yes, I have had the occasional *abuela* (Spanish for grandmother) who doesn't get the idea that special treats need to be *earned* during the training process. But in general, grandparents can be a tremendous asset to the program.

CHOOSING THE SOFTWARE

So, let's say that you have figured out the budget and put together your schedule. Let's go back to Steps One and Two, in which specific software is selected.

As I previously mentioned, when selecting software, I perform an evaluative task that I call Prescriptive Software Selection™. As the name implies, I individually select the correct programs for each individual based on several parameters. By making sure that your child or student receives the right programs, we can optimize the time that is spent on CBI, as well as utilize your resources in the best manner.

I have never believed in a cookie-cutter approach to learning of any sort. I'm sure that most of you have been involved in the Individual Educational Plan (IEP) process somewhere along the line, either for your own child or for your students. Just as the IEP sets individualized goals for each student, the Prescriptive Software Selection™ has the same objective.

In order to select the correct software, there must be a method to determine the level(s) of ability of each person. There are several ways of accomplishing this task. If you have the chance to see a speech and language pathologist either in a private setting or in the school, your child should receive a comprehensive evaluation that will determine the language, speech, and social skill abilities and areas of concern. If not, someone like me can gain the information needed through phone, e-mail, or web-based consultations. Additionally, any psychological tests that may shed some light in the areas of processing, as well as attention and focusing, can be of assistance. Finally, if your child has received any academic evaluations to determine reading and math skills, we can utilize these reports as well.

Incorporating the information from these tests and reports, I can get a fairly accurate picture of where your child is functioning in the areas that the reports have addressed. In many instances, individuals with autism are not able to receive these comprehensive methods of evaluation, either due to logistical constraints or an inability to perform adequately on a standardized test. For these individuals, a comprehensive consultation can give us the information that we need. To be honest, even when I utilize the standardized testing information, I always have additional questions that I must obtain through a consultation with the family and/or caregivers. Tests simply don't tell the complete story.

Once we have enough information, we can proceed to determine at what level your child needs to begin training in the areas selected for the CBI program.

ATTENTION AND FOCUSING AND COMPUTER READINESS

Since I routinely recommend that we begin each CBI session with 15 minutes or so of exercises that are specifically designed to increase the student's level of attention, I think we will start there. This is also the time that we introduce computer readiness skills for individuals who are new to computers. In order to determine which program(s) to utilize, I take many factors into consideration.

First, I need to know if your child has ever used a computer before. If computers are new to him or her, I need to know your child's interests and motivations. For instance, does he like animated characters or music? Is she able to point yet? Does he follow simple directions? Can she sit in a chair, or does she mostly like to jump around? If he can sit, how long can he sit?

For others who have had previous computer experience, I ask if the child can use a mouse or a touchscreen. I want to know which programs your child has used in the past and what he or she enjoyed about them. Conversely, which programs were not successful and why? Does the child have trouble transitioning from one program to another, or is there a tantrum when someone says that computer time is over? How are the child's memory skills? If your child can follow simple directions, how does he or she do with more complex or multi-step directions?

Once we have this information, we select a program that fits the needs of your child. We can determine where we need to begin in terms of readiness and attention and focusing training.

CAUSE AND EFFECT AND LANGUAGE

Many different scales have been utilized to describe language levels. The one that I utilize for CBI is called *Laureate's Linguistic Hierarchy*, and as the name suggests, it was developed by Laureate Learning Systems. The Linguistic Hierarchy illustrates seven stages of language development starting with birth and progressing up to adulthood. These stages can also be used to determine the language level of an individual with language or developmental disabilities.

The first level is called *Interpreted Communication*. In a typically developing individual, it occurs during the first four months of life. The baby demonstrates no direct intention to communicate. They don't understand the fact that they can control their universe through communication to another person. Though this stage usually terminates around the 4-month mark in typical children, it's common for someone with developmental disabilities to stay in this stage until they have received training.

Parents often tell me that their child doesn't communicate wants and needs to them in any way—not verbally or through gestures or pointing. What happens is that the parent or caretaker ends up supplying the child with every need. As you read in Chapter Four, cause and effect skills need to be taught when a child is unable to move forward into the next level.

For typical kids, the next stage occurs somewhere between the fourth and ninth month after birth. This level is called the *Intentional Stage*. Its name implies that the child is now able to demonstrate some ability to signal a caregiver with the intent to communicate. They may use an eye gaze (looking at the item that they want) or gesturing, such as pointing. By the end of this stage, our goal is for the child to be able to comprehend a few spoken words.

The day that we all dream about for our child is the day they reach Stage 3, which is called *Single Words*. As the name implies, the typical child is able to verbalize some words. For those of you who have typical children, you may remember that this experience occurred between nine and eighteen months. For children with autism, the ability to express single words may be accomplished through other means such as sign language, picture communication, or augmentative devices. Regardless of the mode of communication, the ability of a child to express himself or herself through language is a momentous occasion. During this stage, the child develops a core expressive vocabulary from which two-word phrases begin to emerge.

You know that children are in Stage 4 when they use a combination of individual words and a few word combinations to express themselves. This stage is appropriately called *Word Combinations*, and it's usually reached by eighteen to twenty-four months.

Let me take a moment here to discuss exactly what language professionals consider to be true word combinations. The reason that I feel this discussion is necessary is because I often talk with families who tell me that their child is using word combinations. However, upon testing or observation, I notice that the phrases are not word combinations at all but memorized catch phrases that have been taught to them.

Roger Brown, a well known psychologist who developed a structure for analyzing grammatical acquisition in the mid 1970's, describes two-word phrases using 14 different subtypes. Each one of these subtypes describes how each word in the two-word phrase has a separate meaning to the child who uses the phrase. For example, if a child says, "push truck," the child intends to communicate that either they're pushing the truck or want the listener to push the truck. Regardless, the child intends to communicate two separate concepts. The first is that something is being pushed or that they *want* something to be pushed. The second is that the item to be pushed or that they are pushing is the truck.

Compare that example to a more common phrase that is constantly taught by parents and behaviorists: "_____, please." Fill in the blank with any item that the child requests. Though the word "please" has meaning, I often have to ask whether the child really understands what the word means. At this early stage, I highly doubt it. The word "please" is a wonderful word to teach someone to say, but it has a very abstract meaning. Children usually don't learn these abstract meanings until a bit later.

So, if you want to teach your child to say the word "please" after the name of a requested item, go right ahead. It can't hurt, and you should eventually teach it anyway, as it has important social meaning. But understand that it doesn't mean your child is using word combinations just yet. Table 1 shows the phrases that Brown considers to be true two-word combinations.

Table 1 Information provided from Caroline Bowen with permission

Bowen, C. (1998). Speech-language-therapy.com. Retrieved from www. speech-language-therapy.com/ on 06/20/08

Name	Example	What is the intent
Nomination	That book	The item is a book
Recurrence	More juice	The child wants more of something—in this case, juice
Negation (rejection)	No apple	The individual does not want the apple
Negation (denial)	No hitting	The person is denying that they were hitting

Negation (non-existence)	No doggie	May mean that the dog is not here
Agent action	Mommy eat	The child's mother is eating
Action object	Throw ball	The person is either expressing that he wants someone to throw him a ball or someone is actually throwing the ball
Agent object	Boy ball	The boy is performing some action with the ball or indicates that the boy has the ball
Action locative	In car	This identifies the a person is in a car or expresses where the speaker would like to be
Entity locative	dolly bed	Designates where the dolly is or where the person wants the dolly to be
Possessor possession	Baby toy	The toy belongs to the baby
Entity attributive	Blue car (or car blue)	The car in the discussion is blue
Demonstrative entity	That book	The speaker only is referring to a particular book

Each individual acquires these word combinations at different rates, and not all subtypes must be learned before the child moves on to the next stage. But as therapists, teachers, and parents, we strive to teach our children these two-word combinations as they are building blocks to Stage 5: *Early Syntax.*

In Stage 5, which typically occurs between the second and third birthday, the child begins to communicate using a variety of short sentences. Finally, they comprehend questions dealing with the past, such as, "What did you do in school today?" (Many parents I work with complain that their child is unable to answer that question, which appears simple to them. I explain that we have to wait until their child reaches Stage 5.)

This is a wonderful stage, as language really starts to blossom. During this stage, parents feel like they are beginning to truly communicate with their child. The interactive quality of communication is in full swing. The construction of sentences is still fairly rudimentary, but the meaning of the interactions is quite apparent. The next stage, *Syntax Mastery,* leads to the refinement aspects of language.

As the name implies, it's during Stage 6 that the child acquires the bulk of language grammar. They begin this stage with just a handful of sentence structures and exit with most of the syntax (grammar) that they will use. The typical child remains in this stage from the age of three to approximately five years old. By the time a child is five, they are usually communicating in fairly long cohesive paragraphs. By the time the child is ready to exit this stage, you may hear the occasional incorrect verb tense, such as "I runned home," but in general, children are highly effective communicators by this time.

If they're able to reach this stage in their lifetime, our children with developmental disabilities often need far more than the average two years to master all the grammar that they need. And along with the grammar training, we find that this is the stage in which concept development and pragmatic language must be taught.

In the final Stage 7, known as *Complete Generative Grammar*, the typical child, who is five years old and up, is now a fluent speaker and must concentrate on developing the final grammatical structures that will make him or her a proficient communicator. When children leave this stage, they are then ready to develop reading and writing competence. As mentioned in previous chapters, reading and writing skills are intertwined with language development. Obviously, without language comprehension skills, reading comprehension is unattainable. And reading skills are a prerequisite to writing abilities.

In the olden days, children weren't exposed to pre-reading and writing until they went to Kindergarten. (And way back, not until first grade!) Now, children are learning phonics in pre-school, sometimes as early as three years of age. It's not a bad thing—just a sign of our times. It's not unusual for a pre-school teacher to mention to me that one of her students is having trouble understanding phonics. Upon evaluation, I reveal that this particular child isn't even pronouncing his or her sounds correctly. I then have to explain that if the child is unable to pronounce sounds correctly, the child may not be ready to learn phonics for reading.

My point is not that you must wait until a child has perfect language before you begin to teach reading and writing, but instead, you need to have the language art training run parallel in some respects. Training them in this fashion will actually enhance the acquisition of the skills in all areas. Then, once the child has mastered the skills to exit Stage 7 for language development, we can focus on advanced reading and writing competency skills.

Now that I have described the seven levels of language, can you figure out your child's or student's level? If not, I'm just an e-mail or phone call away to help you with this process. Once we determine the level, you can go to my website where you will see the language software categorized by levels. You can then select the correct program for your child with fairly good accuracy. Of course, if you feel uncertain, contact me, and I will help you to make some decisions as to which program(s) are appropriate. I can also help you decide how much time you need to devote to each program. And again, if you have difficulty with scheduling and figuring a budget, call me for that, too. My contact information is in the the back of this book.

SPEECH

The other areas of CBI are a little less complicated to figure out. As I mentioned in the last chapter, in the area of speech and articulation, it is extremely helpful to have a speech pathologist perform a test to determine which sounds or patterns are not produced the way they should be. If you don't have access to a speech therapist, you can have me perform an evaluation online with your child. (Again, I'm able to perform consultations and evaluations of all types using the Internet, which I'll discuss in more detail later.)

Age is a determining factor as well, although a qualified speech pathologist will utilize the language age rather than the chronological age. This means that if your child is six years old but has the language skills of a three-year old, we would expect articulation skills to be somewhere around the three-year old level. We would then recommend articulation training for the sounds that should be produced correctly by the age of three. This is a slightly general statement, as there are times when we may recommend that your child work on a sound that is developed later in order to increase the level of intelligibility. That was the case in the story that follows.

I recently evaluated an eight-year old boy named Shiloh. His parents brought him to me for a speech and language consultation. Shiloh was quite verbal and was using some sentences for communication intent, but he still had a way to go to develop effective language skills. I assessed him to be entering Stage 6 for language. Though Shiloh was chronologically eight years old, I assessed his language age to be at approximately 3-1/2 years. Typically, a child at 3-1/2 doesn't pronounce all of his sounds perfectly. Often, we see mispronunciations with certain sounds (see Table 2 on page __) up until the age of approximately six years. Since Shiloh was speaking like a child of 3-1/2, I would only be concerned with sounds that are supposed to be developed by that time.

It was difficult to understand Shiloh because he mispronounced many words. So, I decided to not only recommend training on the sounds developed at age three and before, but also on a few later developing sounds. I chose the /l/ sound as one of those sounds. This sound is used very frequently in our language, and when it is pronounced correctly, it really boosts the person's level of intelligibility. I recommended other sounds as well.

Once we determine which sounds need training for your child, the selection of programs is relatively simple. You can purchase programs that contain training exercises to improve the production of the sounds that need help. The programs usually contain descriptions of the material that is used for the training. For younger children, I pick programs that have photos and drawings. For older children, however, I only use programs that utilize photos. Also, some of the programs contain fun games, while others are more drill-oriented. Knowing your child and what type of presentation is most motivating will help determine which format will be the most helpful.

Table 2

Ages of Sound Acquisition: Reprinted from website: http://www.lowryspeechtherapy.com/index.htm

p,b,d,t,m,n,w,h	By two years
k,g,f,v,ing,	By four years
s,z,ch,sh,j, l	By five years
r,th	By six years

PHONOLOGICAL PROCESSING

As discussed in Chapter Four, children with autism display phonological processing issues related to auditory processing disorders. We have great phonological processing training programs to help improve these skills. Again, these processes are pattern-oriented rather than sound-oriented. For instance, one pattern is final consonants. We don't break it down by sound like we do for articulation. Like articulation development, however, phonological processes also develop by certain ages.

Table 3 on page __ may be a little technical in nature, but it can help you get a clear picture as to the most common phonological processing issues and at what ages they disappear. We relate the phonological processing age back to the language age as we do with articulation development to determine what processes need training. And just as with articulation, we make exceptions to this rule, especially when we want to greatly improve the child's intelligibility.

Very commonly, children with autism show the processing issue called *final consonant deletion*, where they leave off the final consonant of a word. This issue usually disappears around the age of 3-1/2—just about the same time that a child begins to communicate conversationally. If a child leaves off the last sound of many words, it's extremely difficult for the child to be understood. Consider this sentence: "My da ee uhla uh ha daw." This is a grammatically correct sentence, but I doubt that you can figure out what was said. Here is the translation: "My dad eats a lot of hot dogs." Except for the first word, which ends in a vowel sound, the child left off the last sound or sounds of each word. This is what we mean by *final consonant deletion*.

You can see the huge impact that this can have on a child's ability to be understood. I often recommend working on this process earlier than age 3-1/2. A child with autism who uses only one word really needs that one word to be understood. So, if that child constantly leaves off the last consonant of the word, how effective will that child be in communicating wants and needs? So, it may be important to work on this pattern, as well as other patterns, earlier than the age of disappearance.

Table 3

Process Issue	Example	Approximate age of Disappearance
Weak Syllable Deletion (one of the syllables of a two or more syllable word is left out)	"helicopter" pronounced: "hecopter "	4 years old
Final Consonant Deletion (the final consonant in the syllable is left out)	"hat" Pronounced: "ha"	3 ½ years old
Cluster Reduction (one of the consonants from a blend is omitted)	"spot" Pronounced: "pot"	4 years old

Stopping (a sound that obstructs the airstream, like /t/ or /d/ substituted for a sound that has a continuous airstream like /s/ or /f/	"sun" pronounced: "tun"	3 to 5 years old
Fronting (a sound where the tongue comes forward, like /t/ or /d/ substituted for a sound where the tongue is supposed to go to the back of the mouth, like /k/ or /g/	"cookie" Pronounced: "tootie"	3-1/2 years old
Deaffrication (a sound that combines an obstructed airstream with a continuous airstream, like /ch/ or /j/ changed to a sound that only provides a continuous airstream	"chew" Pronounced: "shoe"	4 to 4-1/2 years old
Gliding (the /l/ or /r/ sounds are replaced with the /w/ or /y/ sound)	"light" Pronounced: "yite"	4 to 5 years old
Devoicing (a sound that vibrates in the larynx like /b/ or /g/ is substituted for the similar sound that doesn't vibrate the larynx like /p/ and /k/)	"bag" Pronounced: "back"	3 years old

As mentioned in the previous chapter, you always want to devote a portion of your computer time to programs specifically geared toward improving attention and focusing. You will see on my website (valerieherskowitz.com) that there are only a handful of programs that are designed to focus specifically on this important training area. So, it's fairly easy to choose. The descriptions of each product will make it simple for you to find the appropriate one.

Social/Pragmatics

You also want to devote a portion of your CBI time to social skill development training (pragmatics) when your child or student is at the developmental age of a pre-schooler. I have developed a chart to help you determine the area in which your child needs to work (Table 4). It's fairly easy to figure out. When your child is very young, focus on the appropriate social skills that need to be utilized in a pre-school environment, another person's home, or in a park or play area, etc. In other words, focus on the skills necessary for the places where your child will be interacting with others. This is the beginning stage of the development of friends.

Later, the school and community are the center of social activity for most individuals, and there are many opportunities for interactions during the course of the day. During this period of a person's life, it's essential that each opportunity is explored and evaluated for pragmatic effectiveness. Most individuals with autism have difficulty in one or more of these areas. Once you have determined where the issue lies, choosing a social skill software program that trains skills in these areas will be fairly simple.

Table 4

Check off all areas in need of training:

Developmental Age	Skill	Needs Training
3-7	Greeting others	
3-7	Listening	
3-7	Interrupting appropriately	
3-7	Sharing	
3-7	Taking turns	
3-7	Following directions	
3-7	Waiting	
3-7	Asking for help	
5-15	Personal safety	
5-15	Using the telephone	
5-15	Joining a group	
5-15	Working cooperatively	
5-15	Showing respect	
5-15	Negotiating	
5-15	Handling frustration	
6-12	Listening	
6-12	Compromising	
6-12	Resolving conflicts	
6-12	Solving problems	
6-12	Dealing with teasing	
6-12	Learning not to be a bully	
6-12	Reasoning	
6-12	Friendship skills	
6-12	Following directions	
6-12	Learning cooperation	

6-12	Following rules	
8-18	Listening	
8-18	Organizing	
8-18	Cooperating	
8-18	Asking for help	
8-18	Personal hygiene	
8-18	Sportsmanship	
8-18	Academic responsibility	
8-18	Self-control	
8-18	Transitioning	
8-18	Time management	
8-18	Following schedules	
10-adult	Shopping skills	
10-adult	Eating out	
10-adult	Using a public restroom	
10-adult	Grocery shopping	
10-adult	Attending appointments	

READING AND LITERACY

As mentioned in the previous chapter, literacy skills are divided into several parts. There are the decoding skills, which are needed to learn to read words through phonics. There is sight word recognition for words that cannot be sounded out. And there are comprehension skills such as answering "wh" questions, understanding the main idea, vocabulary development, and critical thinking. Most of our children with autism will have some level of difficulty in reading comprehension. Some will have across-the-board problems, while others may catch on to the comprehension that involves concrete thinking (like answering direct questions) but will show difficulty with more abstract concepts. Luckily, we have programs that can assist in all of these areas.

Some children may need to start at the beginning. They may not have developed the core skills of reading as of yet. For others, who are a little bit farther along, your child's teacher can be very helpful in letting you know the reading areas where your child needs help. The teacher can tell you the grade level of your child's reading skill, as what skill areas need assistance. I can be of help with this step as well. Often, after just a few short questions, I'm able to determine where we must begin. We have regular software programs that are very helpful, and we also can use computer-based training programs called Fast ForWord® offered by the Scientific Learning Corporation. These programs, which are designed to improve language and literacy skills, are really more like mini-courses that your child or student can enroll in and complete over the Internet. I will elaborate more on these programs in the next chapter.

MATH AND SPELLING

There are a lot of programs that you can purchase at your local computer store which are designed to develop math and spelling skills. The problem with using these programs with our kids is that they aren't designed for them. For the most part, they have been developed to be used with the general population. Therefore, the learning style may not be appropriate for your child.

By learning style, I mean the manner in which every individual learns the best. There are many different learning style models that have been proposed. A common model divides learners into the visual, auditory, or kinesthetic modes. Of course, there are exceptions, but most of our children are visual learners.

As you may expect, a person who learns through the visual modality needs to have visual representations in order to understand certain concepts. For instance, you may have recognized that your child follows directions better when given a small picture as a representation of what needs to be done. We call this technique "following a visual schedule." This method is implemented in most special needs classrooms where children with autism are taught.

Our children learn math and spelling best when visuals are used as well. An example of a visual strategy that is implemented in a math program is the use of counter devices to help teach addition and subtraction. These counters help our children to understand the representation of items that correspond with numbers. Math can be quite abstract at times. But using counters helps make these concepts understandable and concrete.

Therefore, the programs that I usually recommend have been specially developed to teach our children through the visual modality. Many of the individuals I have worked with have finally understood basic math and spelling using these programs.

In order to know where to begin, we must assess whether your child has developed pre-math skills, such as number concepts and counting, or whether the child is farther along. Again, your child's teacher can be quite helpful in determining what skills are needed at this time. Hopefully, you will have a better experience than I had recently. At my son's last IEP meeting, I noticed a very strange goal on his plan. His teacher had specified that Blake would be working on the goal of "making change." Though her intent was honorable (she wanted him to learn a functional skill), I was perplexed (as was the rest of the IEP team) as to why this goal was proposed. Learning to make change would require Blake to be able to do subtraction. In other words, if you hand the cashier a dollar to pay for an item that costs 72 cents, the cashier needs to subtract 72 from 100. Even if the cash register does the subtraction part for the cashier, he still must count 28 cents, which requires addition skills as well as the knowledge of how much each coin is worth.

Of course, I would love for Blake to learn these skills, and I'm hopeful that he will one day. But right now, he is still at the level of matching coins with their value. So, the teacher's goal of "making change" was a little premature. She needs to examine what actual math skills are a pre-requisite for that goal. (It would be great if someone could invent a cash register that tells the cashier which coins or currency to give back to the customer. So, if the customer gives the cashier a twenty dollar bill for an item that costs $5.43, the cash register then tells the cashier to give the customer back one ten dollar bill, four one dollar bills, two quarters, a nickel, and two pennies.)

LIFESKILLS

Teaching lifeskills starts early. As the director of a therapy center, I required each and every one of our therapists to include at least one functional lifeskill in every student's plan of care. The lifeskill that you will choose for your child is not based on age; it's based on ability and motivation. When a child is very young, lifeskills can involve learning to use utensils for eating and drinking, so from a computer-based intervention perspective, I recommend focusing on vocabulary programs that can teach a young child the names of these items (i.e., spoon, fork, cup, etc.) As time progresses, the child may be ready for grooming and dressing skills. Working on the vocabulary for these items is also important, as well as finding the right programs that teach following directions and sequencing for these tasks.

As the child continues to develop, lifeskills will begin to include tasks that are not just about the child, but about the world that the child encounters. At this point, it's essential that your child begin to see him or herself as an integral part of the universe. This universe will include your family life, as well as school. So, training children on the tasks required in these environments will greatly improve their self-esteem.

When my son Blake was about eight, I had just gotten married to my current husband, who has two children from his previous marriage. Together, we had four children—all boys. The age range at the time was 8, 10, 12, and 16. When we got together for family dinners, my husband insisted that each child be given a task. As a matter of fact, he gave one boy the task of washing the dishes, so we never used our dishwasher! Blake had a job as well. He was responsible for setting the table. Once he was trained on the vocabulary words that are used (not just the actual items, but the action words that accompany the items), we began following directions and sequencing training using CBI. Eventually, we began to incorporate the skills into the real life task of setting the table. Within a very short time, Blake was doing his job independently. He relished the opportunity to be involved in a task that involved him in our family life. To this day, he derives a great deal of pride from the tasks that he accomplishes as part of our family unit. He knows that he has a very important place in our world.

Again, as time progresses, lifeskill training will involve more advanced skill sets like telling time and using money, so, obviously, there is a little bit of overlap with the math programs. Remember to always take into consideration the prerequisite skills that need to be trained *before* your child can accomplish a particular skill.

WORKSKILLS

If you think the time to be thinking about work skills is when your child is ready to graduate from high school or college, think again. The preparation for life after school should begin long before that life actually arrives. When I talk about workskills, I'm not just referring to a job for pay that your child may or may not have at the time of graduation. I'm referring to any productive experience that your child engages in as an adult. In the case of my son, Blake, he has spent many years acquiring important abilities in the areas of housekeeping and office skills. He started this process when he was in middle school. At the time of this writing, he is in the 10ᵗʰ grade. He continues to work on new skills and utilize his current skills in real life settings.

He isn't paid for his work, and I don't know if he will ever be compensated financially. But he does work, and I hope and prepare for the day that Blake's skill set will be valued enough that it will warrant payment. Nevertheless, payment isn't the point. The point is productivity.

CBI is a very important component of the training process for life after school. I recommend that your program include workskills once your child is in middle school.

Hardware

Besides selecting software, it's important to decide on the correct hardware. The decisions are fairly uncomplicated, but they're important to the development of a truly effective program. The first important choice is whether your child is ready to use a mouse or whether you need a touchscreen. You can also try the approach where the child touches, and you click. If your child or student is young or a computer novice, your choice should be either a touchscreen or the touch and click method.

One of the problems with the touch and click method, of course, is that most monitors are LCD screens which shouldn't be touched. You can still find CRT monitors, however, which are durable enough to touch. In my office, I always use the touch and click method, since it gives the therapist the most control. Therefore, we use CRT monitors. For a home program application, however, touchscreen overlays are great because they fit over your existing computer monitor. Or you can try the new touchscreen all-in-one computers like HP's Touchsmart or simply their touchscreen monitor.

To take a step back a bit, if you have a child who is still in Stage 1 Language Level and has not established the concept of cause and effect, you may want to consider using a big button switch device. This inexpensive piece of hardware looks like a big round button. All that has to be done to activate it is a light touch to the device. For a child who has difficulty understanding that he or she can make things happen, this button may be the first step. The button is fairly large, which makes access to it very easy. It's also quite appropriate for very young children and those with physical difficulties.

If your child is computer savvy and already using a mouse, you are good to go. I don't usually teach mouse skills at the beginning of CBI, but if your child is already using one, you may as well stick with it. There is an exception, however: There are some programs that are simply more fun with the touchscreen, and you will find that your child is more effective when using the touchscreen with these programs. My son, Blake, for example, is great with a mouse, but he loves to use the touchscreen when he works on certain programs that involve a concentration-type game where he matches pictures together.

I don't know exactly why, but, eventually, most kids learn how to use the mouse fairly easily. I don't really stress over it. For effective CBI, the selection process has to be easy. So, if your child isn't ready for the mouse, stick with the touchscreen or the touch and click approach.

The next question is whether you want to use a desktop or laptop. It doesn't really matter since you can get a touchscreen overlay for a laptop as well. But if your child will be working in multiple locations, a laptop is more convenient.

I do believe that the screen size is important. I like to use bigger screens (17"and up) with these children. I find that having the screen "in your child's face" better captures their attention. And the bigger the better.

The next chapter will be devoted to the software itself. Now that you have a basic understanding of your child's needs, it's time to get a feel for the actual products you will choose from.

Chapter Six: Think Questions and Activities:

1. Go to the back of the book, and fill out the CBI Budget.

2. Then, complete the CBI Scheduler, also at the back of the book.

3. If you have any issues with budget or scheduling, set up a consultation with Valerie to help you with this step.

4. Go through the language stages above and determine to the best of your ability which stage you believe your child or student currently falls within. Next, go to the website, valerieherskowitz.com, and visit the software store. Click on language programs, followed by the stage you have determined for your child. You will find some appropriate programs there to begin your CBI program in language.

5. Next, refer to the list of skill areas that you developed from the activities in the last chapter. You can then go to valerieherskowitz. com and select items you feel are appropriate using the information from this chapter.

6. As an alternative, you can schedule an appointment with Valerie to help you select your child's programs.

CHAPTER SEVEN:

SO LET'S TALK SOFTWARE

"Be nice to nerds. Chances are you'll end up working for one."

-Bill Gates

I won't go into detail about each program (which would make this book longer than *War and Peace*), but I will give you a little bit of information about the companies that have developed the products. (I will also include links in the Appendix for you to obtain more information about the products of interest.) I don't want to use this information as a selling tool but just to give you a little background.

As I wrote this chapter, it was interesting to discover that every single manufacturer went into the software development business with more of a desire to improve the lives of those with special needs than to build a profitable business. So, I will go out on a limb to say that the individuals who have been involved in software development are people with a great interest in our children.

LAUREATE LEARNING SYSTEMS

The name Laureate is synonymous with language software. It was back in 1982 when the team of Dr. Mary Sweig-Wilson and Mr. Bernard Fox joined forces to bring technology to the special needs community. There programs were based on the research that they had completed on micro-computer language intervention. Since that time, Laureate Learning Systems has developed over 60 programs. There is no doubt that their programs are the cornerstone for language development for our kids. As I referenced in the last chapter, they developed the Linguistic Hierarchy, which is the basis for the seven stages of language acquisition and the method that I use to select the appropriate language programs for each individual.

Over the last several years, Laureate has redesigned many of its existing programs to include a new type of technology called Optimized Intervention™. This system allows the individual to progress automatically at his or her own rate. In other words, the material adjusts as the child makes gains. This technology makes CBI exceptionally user-friendly for home programs. In the "olden days," I worked with families to make manual adjustments to the features on the programs as the child's needs changed. But now, with Optimized Intervention™, the need for consultative services is greatly reduced.

James is a young boy with autism from Northern Saskatchewan who discovered the Laureate programs when he was four years old. Up until that time, only James' parents knew how smart he was. Though he was able to sign many words to express himself, his verbal vocabulary was extremely limited. As a result, many teachers were unable to recognize James' innate intelligence. Then one summer day in a random Internet search, James' mother, Cindy, found the Laureate programs. Immediately, she became excited about trying computer-based learning with her son.

After a brief consultation, Cindy selected programs from Stage Two. She felt that this was the right starting point for James. As Cindy reports, from the moment James began to utilize the programs, his focusing, attention, and motivation all increased dramatically. Cindy realized her son and computer-based training were a great marriage.

In the past, James had been quite reluctant to sit at a table and work on language development. He was all over the place. But the computer excited him enough that he paid attention for long periods of time. Within just 2-1/2 weeks, James' expressive verbal vocabulary increased by 150%. He began to verbally utilize all of the words he learned from the software programs, and he often called others to the computer in order to demonstrate his abilities.

Finally, his teachers were able to see his great intelligence. Even his parents were shocked by certain developments. One day, they inadvertently turned off the sound on the computer. Much to their surprise, James was able to continue the program without the sound by reading the sentences on the bottom of the screen. Up until that time, no one had any idea that James was able to read.

James' mother, Cindy, feels that these programs have been the best resource they have ever found. Cindy has said, "Computer training has opened the door for James to learn." He quickly moved from Stage Two programs into Stage Three and is continuing to make huge strides in his language development.

LocuTour by Learning Fundamentals

Often, new products are developed when a particular need is established. So goes the story with LocuTour software programs that are marketed by Learning Fundamentals. In 1994, a speech pathologist was trying to utilize the existing software for her clients with brain injuries and autism. She felt that the available software programs in DOS-based formats were just not meeting her patient's needs. So, Myrna Scarry-Larkin and her brother, John Scarry, began to develop their own line of remedial software. They started with a program for improving focusing, memory, and attention skills and eventually branched out to include speech, language, and reading-based software.

Most people involved with autism in one way or another, whether a parent or professional, would agree that many individuals with autism are drawn to trains. Myrna recognized this interest and developed a language program targeted for the autism population that is all about trains. The program is for the higher language individual and utilizes photos and vocabulary.

SOCIAL SKILL BUILDER

Again, product followed need for two speech pathologist sisters, Laurie and Jennifer Jacobs. They had a background in treating individuals with autism, and they discovered a need for technology to improve the social skills of the autism population. They started Social Skill Builder in 1999 in order to create these programs. Their software uses interactive video sequences in real life scenarios to teach appropriate social behavior to individuals with autism.

THE ATTAINMENT COMPANY

The Attainment Company, which was founded in 1979, started by developing curriculum to assist special needs individuals to succeed in the work and school settings. Dan Bastian, the founder and CEO, started his company when he was a program coordinator for a Wisconsin rehabilitation agency.

The Attainment Company has a plethora of products that focus on functional development. They frequently collaborate with the University of North Carolina at Charlotte in the development of new products that are used with the autism population.

ANIMATED SPEECH CORPORATION

Back in November of 2001 (I remember this date since it occurred right after 9/11), I was asked to work with Cure Autism Now in setting up a technology conference in Menlo

Park, California. At that time, we featured a speaker named Dr. Dom Massaro. Along with his colleague, Dr. Michael Cohen, Dr. Massaro was analyzing how visual perception affects the ability of individuals to understand what a speaker is communicating. In order to pursue this research, they developed an animated talking head named Baldi®, whose facial muscles and speech articulators moved with excellent accuracy.

Eventually, Dr. Massaro teamed up with Dan Feshbach, a parent of a child with autism and the CEO of a financial technology corporation. Together, they started the Animated Speech Corporation. Their products focus on conversational learning systems featuring animated talking tutors. Eventually, the character of Baldi® became Timo, who engages children by calling them by name. He also navigates them through the individualized lessons in these programs.

JIGSAW LEARNING COMPANY AND TEACHTOWN, INC.

Recently, Animated Speech Corporation teamed up with another software manufacturer to create the Jigsaw Learning Company. This other software manufacturer, TeachTown, Inc., was founded by a psychologist named Dr. Chris Whalen. I share the same belief with Dr. Whalen: That children with autism are extremely motivated by computer-based learning. Along with her team of expert designers and video game developers, Dr. Whalen has developed software products that are based on sound clinical research and include the fun factor as well.

ACCELERATIONS EDUCATIONAL SOFTWARE

One day, Karl Smith, an engineer and software developer, as well as the father of a son with autism, decided that he needed to put all of his talents together to develop a product that would function as an effective and cost-efficient method for training children like his son. He felt that in order for these individuals to learn, they needed an individualized approach. For this reason, he started Accelerations Educational Software.

He has designed software to be compatible with one-to-one learning, and as the mission of the company states, the software was developed for even the lower functioning individual. The company's product uses behavioral methodology as the basis for the training approach, which Karl discovered was extremely beneficial for his own child. Since hours of one-to-one training with a live person is extremely effective but also expensive, his goal has been to offer a product that emulates this experience in a computer-based format in order to give families the "biggest bang for the buck."

Chapter Seven: Think Questions and Activities:

1. Now that you have put together your budget, scheduled in the time, and either selected some programs or worked with Valerie, it's time to order the programs, if you haven't done so already.

2. The next step is to set up a lesson plan for each of the activity sessions. We have included one at the back of the book. If you need help with this process, Valerie can help you.

3. So, here you are with everything in place. Get started!

4. After two weeks, you may want to tweak your lesson plan a bit. Lesson planning is an ongoing activity, not something you do just once.

5. After a few months, you may need to order some new programs, as your child will hopefully have progressed.

6. Congratulations!! You now have a successful CBI program.

CHAPTER EIGHT:

AUGMENTATIVE COMMUNICATION

"Communication leads to community, that is, to understanding, intimacy and mutual valuing."
-Rollo May

No book or article on technology for individuals with autism would be complete without a significant amount of information on alternative and augmentative communication. Without assistive technology, many individuals with autism would not have an ability to communicate. We call this area AAC.

AAC is often recommended when a person doesn't develop the ability to communicate verbally, but it's also utilized as a tool for speakers who need assistance with certain aspects of communication. For example, children who use AAC have shown a great deal of improvement in many areas, including behavior, attention, and social skills. This makes sense since many children become frustrated when they can't communicate.

I will never forget the day that I made the decision to move ahead with AAC for Blake. We were in a grocery store, and Blake threw a huge fit when I couldn't understand what product he wanted me to buy. Once we started to utilize augmentative communication strategies, Blake's frustration reduced significantly. AAC can also help children in academic areas.

Many people have the misconception that AAC can impede verbal language development. A common question from parents is: "Won't my child become dependent on his device rather than try to speak?" But this is not the case, and research backs up the claim that AAC often improves the acquisition of speech rather than the opposite.

Nothing bothers me as much as when I see a child (or an adult for that matter) who is locked in his or her own head with little or no systematic method to extend thoughts to the outside world. The closest most of us come to experiencing this frustration is when we visit a foreign country and have no ability to communicate in the native language.

I had this experience when I visited Prague about 20 years ago when it was still under the Soviet regime. During my very first day, I got lost. I had absolutely no idea where I was and no way to contact anyone (this was before cell phones), and I was struck with sheer terror. I remember standing in the middle of the city for several minutes while I experienced the panic. Finally, I made my way to a merchant where I was able to write down the name of my hotel followed by a question mark. The merchant, who was thankfully able to comprehend my dilemma, drew me a map in order for me to find my way back. This exchange of information was accomplished in its entirety through non-verbal communication, as neither of us spoke the other's language. My visual skills for directions are simply pathetic, so making my way back to the hotel was no simple feat, but I did arrive safe and sound, even though I was frustrated and exhausted from the experience.

Of course, I was able to write down the name of my hotel and interpret the map given to me by the merchant. These abilities are not necessarily shared by non-verbal individuals with autism. In fact, such abilities are rare with this group. So, if one of these individuals were lost in the same kind of circumstance, the situation would be far more serious.

My son, Blake, was once put on a school bus that was driven by a substitute driver. This person was unfamiliar with the bus route and, for some reason, didn't have our address. Instead of calling the dispatcher, the bus driver spent several hours attempting to find our home. Finally, she called the appropriate individuals and made her way to us. Of course, I was frantic by then. Interestingly, my son is able to write his name, address, and phone number, but no one bothered to ask him. Now, he wears an I.D. bracelet with my cell phone number on it, and his augmentative device also includes our address.

Countless times, I have encountered individuals who have thoughts in their head but are unable to communicate those thoughts outwardly. Somehow, some way, we must find their thoughts and help them bring those thoughts to the surface. Whether it's through sign language, picture systems, voice devices, or a combo approach, our goal is to assist them to communicate.

As you may remember from Chapter Two, my son, Blake, was in this category. Without the ability to utilize technology, he would have spent his entire life trying to get me to understand what he wanted. Augmentative communication is a huge part of his life.

There's a wonderful song by the Moody Blues called, "I Know You Are Out There Somewhere." Whenever I hear it, I cry like a river. The lyrics of the chorus remind me of our children and our hope of finding them and bringing them back "home."

> *"I know you're out there somewhere*
> *Somewhere, somewhere*
> *I know I'll find you somehow*
> *And somehow I'll return again to you."*

When I think about augmentative communication, I think about how it is to be utilized to "find" our children—to give them a path to deliver their messages to us.

Basically, augmentative or alternative communication is divided into high, mid, low, and no tech systems. No tech systems are like the Picture Exchange Communication System (PECS) and sign language. In other words, these are non-technological systems. Usually, PECS is used as a precursor to the higher tech devices, but not always. Computer literacy is also a great way to develop the prerequisites for these systems.

Low tech devices usually offer the user only one, two, or four choices, while mid-tech equipment offers many choices, but does not include the ability to change screens. High tech machines include the technology of the dynamic screen.

A SUCCESS STORY

Pedro, a five-year old boy with autism, recently came to my center for Auditory Integration Training (AIT). While he received this service, his mother and I had a great deal of time to speak. (AIT runs 10 hours over a two-week period.) By the end of the time, I had gotten to know Pedro fairly well. What I learned was that he was extremely bright but also very frustrated because he couldn't communicate. I spoke to his mother about PECS, but she told me that they had tried it rather unsuccessfully. (He liked to chew on the cards.)

I helped Pedro's mother create a picture system that eliminated the individual cards, but I decided it was time to start Pedro on the path of technology. So, I recommended that the family begin a home-based computer intervention program. We chose an array of language programs and included one series designed to teach expressive language skills through augmentative communication.

Pedro's mother called me the very next day after their package of software arrived. "Pedro has taken to the software like he was born to it," she reported. "He constantly requests to work on the computer and is in love with the program that trains the expressive language skills."

Within weeks, Pedro was ready to try a device. We chose one that complimented his present skills but still allowed for growth. Though Pedro is still at the beginning stages of utilizing this device, his skills are light years ahead of others who haven't had his computer experience. He is already able to ask to use the machine, and his level of frustration has reduced considerably.

THE VARIOUS AUGMENTATIVE DEVICES

Some devices use technology called Speech Output. Some provide the voice through digitized speech (someone records their voice into the machine) or synthesized speech (electronic speech.) There are others that use pre-recorded messages.

Many companies provide these augmentative devices, and the following information is just an overview of some of these companies, as well as their products. In no way are the following explanations intended to be utilized as a measure for selecting the right device for your child. In the Appendix, you will find the websites for these companies. It is definitely recommended that you have your child evaluated by a specialist who works with this type of equipment before you purchase one of these devices. Your child's school system probably uses one of these devices, but a word of caution: Make sure you become familiar with these devices before you allow the school to decide which one is right for your child.

Too often, I have been called because the device that the school personnel have selected is inappropriate. Sometimes, it's chosen simply because the school's budget doesn't allow for a more expensive device. Of course, if your child has become computer savvy, the school's personnel may grossly underestimate your child's abilities. This is where I can come into the mix if you so desire and lead you in the right direction.

Note: The following information is based on what was available in 2008. By the time you read this section, there may be upgrades or changes to the equipment mentioned below.

DYNAVOX

Blake's machine is manufactured by a company called DynaVox. Their equipment offers a dynamic screen display (high tech), which means that the individual touches one of the buttons on the screen, and this action brings up a new page. Therefore, there are endless opportunities for pictures. If a button says "foods," for example, you can program the machine to bring up several food items on a new screen when the button is pushed. On that new page, you may have another button that says "fruits." By pushing that button, *another* page comes up with all of the fruits. This layering of pages is individually programmed to meet the needs of the person using the device. This type of technology works really well for an individual who has great visual memory skills (as many of people with autism do.)

The speech output on Blake's device is synthesized. It gives us a choice of voice. As he gets older, I have been changing the voice to correspond with his age. His device also offers a keyboard page that allows a sophisticated user the option to type their thoughts. It uses word prediction (where the device anticipates the word you want to type when you just type in the first few letters), which is a very helpful tool.

Blake's device, called a Dynamite, and isn't manufactured anymore. It has been replaced by the new DynaVox V series, which I'm currently trying to get for Blake. The new upgrade has many more features on it that I feel would benefit Blake. For instance, they offer software called InterAACT®, which sets specific vocabulary that compliments a user's age and communication abilities. This way, Blake would have pages on the device that would help him communicate more efficiently within specific environments and contexts.

DynaVox manufactures the M3, which uses digitized speech (you record your voice into the machine.) This device is appropriate for a child with emergent language. It offers a more simple presentation than that of the DynaVox V. When using a digitized voice device, it's best to record a person who is similar in age to the child.

This device can also present different scenes on the screen, making it quite easy for young children to use it. If you're at the park, for example, you can load the scene of the park on the box, which will allow all words associated with the park to be accessed quickly.

ZYGO INDUSTRIES

Devices from Zygo Industries, which has been around for quite awhile, are divided into several types. They offer mid-tech digital recording equipment (you record your voice into the machine) with overlays that you change as needed. One of the devices is called the Talara. It's an entry level machine, while the other line, called the Macaw, has a lot more storage space for additional communicative opportunities. These devices are good for individuals without the ability to use a dynamic screen. They are also a lot less expensive, costing hundreds rather than thousands of dollars, like the dynamic screen types. Zygo has also a line of dynamic screen devices, however, which are called the Optimist.

Prentke Romich

Another company that offers the dynamic screen is Prentke Romich, which is well-known in the industry. They make the Vanguard Plus device, which offers both digitized and synthesized speech. Their Springboard line is for emergent communicators and is available in English and Spanish.

Their newest device, the ECO-14, is really great. It combines a voice device with Windows computing. (I may have to look into this one for Blake.) With just a push of a button, you can change from speech device to computing. One thing I really like about this company is that they offer a training seminar called LAMP for speech pathologists to learn how to teach functional communication with AAC.

Words+

Words+ offers a line of products called Say-it! SAM. Their tablet-sized dynamic screen device is only four pounds and fairly rugged. They also offer a small, hand-held device with the same software. New to Words+ is a device called Tuff Talker Convertible. This lightweight 6-lb. machine switches from communicator to Windows computer in a similar way to the ECO-14. Obviously, a piece of equipment that includes both a speech device and a computer is optimal.

Saltillo

The Saltillo company is known for their PDA-type device called ChatPC. Since its inception in 2000, they have added new features and now offer the 4th version (ChatPC-4). It contains a very functional vocabulary system to help individuals make sentences for communication. The device is rugged in design and incorporates new synthesized voice technology that is more natural sounding. Saltillo also makes lower cost devices called ChatBox, which have static screens (not dynamic) and are tablet-sized. These are good for emergent communicators.

Though there are many commonalities among devices, there are distinct differences as well. And these differences can make or break your success. That's why it's very important that you have a professional work with you to not only choose the right device, but to train your child, you, and your child's entire staff in the programming and use of the equipment. I have seen many children with the wrong machine or, in some cases, the correct one but no one to train everyone properly.

Each device uses a different set of pictures as icons for the words. It's important to recognize whether your child can associate the type of visuals that are included in a specific device. It's also important that you have a trial period before your child commits to a particular device.

Low tech devices are sometimes necessary in the very beginning of the augmentative communication journey. There are big button types, which just communicate one message, as well as others that convey from 2-16 thoughts. Companies that manufacture these types are AbleNet, Enabling Device, Satillo, and Mayer Johnston.

Getting involved with a device can be overwhelming. Most individuals will contact their speech pathologist first, thinking that this person will lead them in the right direction. I wish I had a nickel, however, for every speech pathologist without the necessary background to adequately recommend or train an individual for the correct equipment. Augmentative communication is a very specialized field, and you must find someone who is qualified to help you with the selection process.

Again, as I have mentioned before, your school district should have someone who is uniquely trained in this area. If they are the helpful type, you will be lucky to have them help you select a device for your child. There will be assessment procedures that will need to be accomplished first, of course. Unfortunately, my own personal experiences with the public school augmentative communication personnel have been less than optimal. I know there are wonderful ones out there (I have met many of them), but many of the dealings I've had—both for my own child and for children I've worked with—have been a nightmare. I know that they have budgets to work with and that the more advanced devices are expensive. But this often means that the device recommended isn't the best one for the child. I can't stress enough how important it is to be educated before you allow the system to make decisions for your child. So, log on to the websites provided at the end of the book and/or contact me when you want to start this process.

There are sometimes other channels for securing your child's devices as well. Some insurance companies, including Medicaid, have purchased equipment when it is proven to be medically necessary. If you can do it, purchasing a device on your own is very liberating because it puts you in the driver's seat. Just make sure that you have someone on your child's support team to help you fully utilize the device. Nothing is sadder than spending lots of money on a piece of equipment that collects dust in the closet or isn't correctly used, especially when it can be so beneficial for your child when utilized properly.

Chapter Eight: Think Questions and Activities:

1. Think about whether or not your child is communicating effectively. If the answer is, "no," continue to the next think question.

2. Has your child ever tried a voice output system? If the answer is "yes," is this device working? If not, or if you answered "no" to the first question, proceed to the next question.

3. Log onto the websites to read more about the devices listed in this book.

4. Think about whether your child should use a low, mid, or high tech device. (Contact me if you have trouble determining this.)

5. Contact your school personnel, and arrange an augmentative communication assessment.

6. Before attending the meeting to find out the results of the assessment, be sure to ask which device they recommend. This way, if it conflicts with what you have in mind, you will be prepared to defend your opinion.

Chapter Nine:

A Better Future for Our Kids

There is no doubt in my mind that technology offers individuals with autism golden opportunities for learning, communication, and a better life. For many parents who have felt that their children would always stay locked in their own worlds, technology has been the key that has opened the door. I have seen it happen many, many times.

I hope that many of you will contact me to begin a CBI program with your child or student. The rewards are enormous. Wherever your child falls on the spectrum and whether your child has ever used a computer before, the programs currently on the market and in development can bring about the kind of positive change that you may have never thought possible.

If money is an issue for your family, consider that home-based CBI programs are less expensive than therapy. It is a very cost-effective and economical way to help your child. Even if the cost of a home-based program is still difficult for you, there are options available. Don't let economic fears stand in your way. You owe it to your child, your family, and yourself to explore the possibilities. It will no doubt save money, time, and stress in the future, as your child achieves greater independence.

The companies profiled in this book and in the Appendix are devoted to creating more and more effective devices and software for individuals with autism. Considering the strides that have already been made, it's exciting to think about what will be available to our children in the future. Disney's "Dream Home of Innoventions" is just the beginning, and we owe it to our children and students to use everything available to us to help them live productive and fulfilling lives.

CBI Financial Planning Worksheet

Proposed Budget for the Program:

ITEM	COST
Initial Consultation	
Software	
Personnel	
Initial Training	
Periodic Training Updates	

   I.   **Resources for Consultation:**

       A. Self: _____

       B. Family: _____

       C. Friends: _____

       D. School: _____

       E. Fundraising: _____

       F. Other: _____

   II.   **Resources for the Software:**

       A. Self: _____

       B. Family: _____

       C. Friends: _____

       D. School: _____

       E. Fundraising: _____

       F. Other: _____

  III.   **Resources for Personnel:**

       A. Self: _____ per _____

       B. Family: _____ per _____

       C. Friends: _____ per _____

       D. School: _____ per _____

       E. Fundraising: _____ per _____

       F. Other: _____ per _____

IV.　Resources for Initial Training:
　　A.　Self: _____
　　B.　Family: _____
　　C.　Friends: _____
　　D.　School: _____
　　E.　Fundraising: _____
　　F.　Other: _____

V.　Resources for Periodic Training Updates:
　　A.　Self: _____ per _____
　　B.　Family: _____ per _____
　　C.　Friends: _____ per _____
　　D.　School: _____ per _____
　　E.　Fundraising: _____ per _____
　　F.　Other: _____ per _____

CBI Scheduler

Instructions:

1. Make a copy of this scheduler.

2. With a red pen, write down all of the activities for your child that do not change from week to week.

3. Next, with a black pen, cross out any times that are not available due to your own commitments.

4. Next, with a green pen, schedule in a minimum of three times a week that your child can devote to CBI. Don't worry if you don't use the entire hour for this activity. Also, include the name of the person who will be working with your child, i.e.: you, your spouse, a caretaker, a home program trainer, a grandparent, a sibling, etc.

5. Make several copies of the scheduler with the red, black, and green entries on it.

6. Each week, use a new sheet and add in your child's schedule for the week in pencil.

7. Block out any times that are not available during the week due to your own commitments.

8. Now, add in extra time that you can devote to CBI during this week.

Monday

Time	Activity
7:00 AM	
8:00 AM	
9:00 AM	
10:00 AM	
11:00 AM	
12:00 PM	
1:00 PM	
2:00 PM	
3:00 PM	
4:00 PM	
5:00 PM	
6:00 PM	
7:00 PM	
8:00 PM	

Tuesday

Time	Activity
7:00 AM	
8:00 AM	
9:00 AM	
10:00 AM	
11:00 AM	
12:00 PM	
1:00 PM	
2:00 PM	
3:00 PM	
4:00 PM	
5:00 PM	
6:00 PM	
7:00 PM	
8:00 PM	

Wednesday

Time	Activity
7:00 AM	
8:00 AM	
9:00 AM	
10:00 AM	
11:00 AM	
12:00 PM	
1:00 PM	
2:00 PM	
3:00 PM	
4:00 PM	
5:00 PM	
6:00 PM	
7:00 PM	
8:00 PM	

Thursday

Time	Activity
7:00 AM	
8:00 AM	
9:00 AM	
10:00 AM	
11:00 AM	
12:00 PM	
1:00 PM	
2:00 PM	
3:00 PM	
4:00 PM	
5:00 PM	
6:00 PM	
7:00 PM	
8:00 PM	

Friday

Time	Activity
7:00 AM	
8:00 AM	
9:00 AM	
10:00 AM	
11:00 AM	
12:00 PM	
1:00 PM	
2:00 PM	
3:00 PM	
4:00 PM	
5:00 PM	
6:00 PM	
7:00 PM	
8:00 PM	

Saturday

Time	Activity
7:00 AM	
8:00 AM	
9:00 AM	
10:00 AM	
11:00 AM	
12:00 PM	
1:00 PM	
2:00 PM	
3:00 PM	
4:00 PM	
5:00 PM	
6:00 PM	
7:00 PM	
8:00 PM	

Sunday

Time	Activity
7:00 AM	
8:00 AM	
9:00 AM	
10:00 AM	
11:00 AM	
12:00 PM	
1:00 PM	
2:00 PM	
3:00 PM	
4:00 PM	
5:00 PM	
6:00 PM	
7:00 PM	
8:00 PM	

MAKE COPIES OF THIS PLANNER

Day _____

Program	Length of Time	Result

Day _____

Program	Length of Time	Result

APPENDIX

Accelerations Educational Software
http://www.dttrainer.com

Animated Speech Corporation (Animated Language Learning Systems)
http://www.animatedspeech.com/

Attainment Company
http://www.attainmentcompany.com

Jigsaw Learning Company
http://www.jigsaw.org

Laureate Learning Systems
http://www.laureatelearning.com

Learning Fundamentals (LocuTour)
http://www.learningfundamentals.com

Social Skill Builder
http://www.socialskillbuilder.com

TeachTown, Inc.
http://www.teachtown.com

BIBLIOGRAPHY

1. Dawson , G., & Zanolli, K (2003). Early intervention and brain plasticity in autism. In G. Bock & J. Goode (Eds.), 2003 *Autism: neural basis and treatment possibilities. Wiley, Chichester (Novaritis Foundation Symposium 251)* (pp. 266-280). Chichester, UK: John Wiley & Sons Ltd.

2. Mundkur, N (2005). Neuroplasticity in Children., *Indian Journal of Pediatrics, 2005; 72 (10)*

3. Bowen, C. (1998). Speech-language-therapy dot com. Retrieved from www.speech-language-therapy. com/ on 06/20/08

4. http://www.lowryspeechtherapy.com/index.htm

5. http://www.personal.psu.edu/mam1034/csd300. phonologicalprocesses.html

ABOUT THE AUTHOR

Visit http://www.ValerieHerskowitz.com for a wealth of information about CBI programs. Register for our CBI Webinar, download free articles, and visit our software store and blog.

Feel free to contact Valerie at (954) 236-9415 to ask any questions you may have and to ask for assistance in developing your child's home-based CBI program.

BIO OF VALERIE HERSKOWITZ, MA CCC-SLP

One of the world's foremost speakers on the subject of computer-based intervention with special needs individuals, Valerie Herskowitz is President of the non-profit organization the National Autism Registry and serves on the advisory board of US Autism & Asperger Association.

She is also founder of the Dimensions Therapy Center, which provides special private therapy services and special events around the South Florida area for families with special needs. She has expanded her computer-based intervention for families and professionals on a national scale by establishing a "global autism support village" through, webcasts, teleconferencing and other cyber tools as well as individual consulting.

Valerie's career as a speech pathologist spans over 30 years. A recipient of the Stevie Lifetime Achievement Award for her work with autistic and special needs children, she has also been honored for starting two innovative community programs, Mothers of Special Needs Individuals (MOSI) and the Dimensions Family Club.

Her youngest son, Blake, was diagnosed in 1993 with autism. Her professional journey as a therapist and as a parent of an autistic child have combined to give Valerie the unique insights to help families cope with problems they face in parenting a child with autism. She is also a contributing writer for a number of national publications on the subject of autism.

Affiliations:

President: National Autism Registry (NARY)

Vice President: Association for Developmentally-Disabled Adolescents And Adults (AFDDAA)

Advisory Board: United States Autism and Asperger Association (USAAA)

Member of: Florida Speech, Language, and Hearing Association (FLASHA), American Speech, Language and Hearing Association (ASHA), International Coaching Federation (ICF), International Association of Coaches (IAC), ADHD Coaching Organization (ACO), National Study Group on Chronic Disorganization (NSGCD), and National Association of Professional Organizers (NAPO)

Made in the USA
Lexington, KY
07 March 2011